# DAVID LEATHERBERRY

# *Julie,* MY LOVE

# RECOMMENDATIONS

Genuine, courageous, and sometimes bold, Julie shows us what it truly means to be a faithful servant in the Kingdom of God. Her unshakeable faith in the Lord, her unwavering compassion for those God called her to serve, and her steadfastness in following His plan are an example and inspiration to women and men alike. Julie and David are loving partners and companions who have always kept Christ at the center of their marriage. Together they have joyfully brought the Lord's gospel and His love to countless people, always giving glory to God regardless of the circumstances they faced.

*Sierra Maxwell,* mother of three, elementary school teacher, Rutland, Vermont

For three years God blessed me with the opportunity to daily witness this godly love story. *Julie, My Love* is a precious pearl and valuable blueprint for young couples seeking to have Christ at the center of their marriages. The book is full of amazing examples of what God designed marriage to look like. I thank the Lord for the privilege of joining the many who call Julie and David their spiritual parents.

*Donnie Bostwick,* former head basketball coach, Southwestern Assemblies of God University

As evident from the very beginning, Julie's unwavering commitment to God and her husband, David, was based on a firm foundation. Their unmovable dedication to each other enabled the roots of their love to grow deeper and their marriage to blossom. After 54 years of close friendship with Julie, I can attest to the beauty of their marriage. If you want to know how that came about, you will find the answer in *Julie, My Love*.

*Judy Neuman,* pastor's wife, Crown Point, Indiana

As a university student, from the first day I met pastor David and Julie, David's love for his radiant wife was clearly evident. The blending of their different temperaments, while still being distinctly themselves, has been beautiful to see as together they pursued God's purpose for their lives. Reading their love story will inspire a husband and wife to cherish, protect, and nurture their own unique relationship.

*Michael Aemmer,* retired family and marriage counselor, Phoenix, Arizona

*Julie, My Love* is one woman's journey of humble obedience to the God she loves. The book is authentic and heartfelt. These stories challenge me to break out of my comfort zone by taking steps of faith, and then seeing the mighty hand of God at work in my own life.

*Deborah Landis,* businesswoman, Canfield, Ohio

Julie lives a life full of adventure with God and her husband David. It amazes me how Julie, at any age, is ready to go anyplace regardless of how challenging the situation may be. As you read *Julie, My Love* your own heart will be filled with faith.

*Annisa Morton,* mother of seven, homemaker, Strafford, Missouri

David's snapshots from Julie's life have captured portraits of a remarkable godly woman. I was blessed to witness firsthand Julie's grace, because as a single person I lived overseas with David and Julie for extended periods of time. Their marriage caused me to earnestly desire for my own marriage their priceless treasure: a lifetime of deep mutual trust, genuine and lasting love, and joyous obedience to God.

*Joshua Payne,* father of three who resides and ministers in a sensitive country

# Julie, MY LOVE

## David Leatherberry

ENHEARTEN
BOOKS

**Julie, My Love**
By David Leatherberry

Edited by Rollene Storms

Printed in the United States of America
ISBN: 979-8-88955-293-2
Copyright 2023, David Leatherberry

Published by Enhearten Books, Springfield, Missouri

Cover Design and Interior Layout by Jennifer Hall

Unless otherwise indicated, all Scripture references
are from the Holy Bible New International Version,
@1984, Zondervan Bible Publishers.

Some narratives are adapted from the author's books
*Afghanistan, My Tears* and *Abdul and Mr. Friday*.

Dedicated
*to*
Joe and Jenny Stevens
*and*
Reverend William and Miriam Uncapher
*who*
laid a firm foundation in Julie's life

# ACKNOWLEDGMENTS

It takes a dedicated team to birth a book that will have lasting value. I am greatly indebted to the following persons:

*Rollene Storms,* a gifted editor who is delightful to work with because of her patience, insights, and marvelous sense of humor. This book could never have been what it should be without her expertise.

*Carol Nichols,* whose valuable suggestions wonderfully enhanced this book.

*Jeannie Royer,* a faithful friend and our superb and leading proofreader.

*Jennifer Hall,* a very gracious and creative book cover designer and interior formatter.

*Don Cain,* who wisely advised me regarding publication.

*Ken Horn* and *Phyllis Freeman,* remarkable authors in their own right, who constantly encouraged me.

*Ricky Spindler,* lead pastor of Stone Creek Church in Urbana, Illinois, who went beyond the extra mile to encourage me to write this book.

# FOREWORD

I am honored that David asked me to write the
foreword of this book about his wife Julie. I met
this amazing couple in the 1980s when I was preparing
to serve in Pakistan. Our friendship extends over many
years, on different continents, and through different
seasons of life.

Julie is an incredible friend: wise, thoughtful,
generous, and encouraging. Her abiding peace, humor
and enthusiasm for life are contagious. She exudes joy
and knows how to bring out the best in people.

Julie's God-given gifts of administration, organizational
ability, practicality, and homemaking enhance their
marriage and balance their ministry as a couple.

She is a remarkable woman who has lived a life
of firm faith in some of the most challenging places
on earth, under arduous circumstances, yet with joy
and creativity while gladly yielding to the will of God.
When Julie believes she and David have heard from the
Lord, nothing holds her back! She packs up and goes,
without looking back!

This inquisitive lady loves to learn. She constantly
delves into the Bible, reads thought-provoking books,
and enjoys carrying on meaningful conversations. She
has a close walk with God and is a woman of prayer.

Julie adapted to cross-cultural life wherever she lived.
She makes friends and shares her life in practical ways.
When living in an Islamic country she gracefully adapted

to restrictions of acceptable behavior and dress. For two years she lived in Kandahar, Afghanistan, under the fanatical Taliban, forbidden to speak with other women. Yet Julie was content because she believed God had given her this assignment.

Whether she is working with Afghan refugees in camps or veterans in Russia, encouraging refugees in Macedonia or Yazidis in Iraq, or mentoring college students called to missions, Julie's enthusiasm for life overflows to those around her.

Who should read this book? Single women and men, those contemplating marriage, husbands and wives, missionaries serving cross-culturally, and those who want their faith strengthened.

You will enjoy reading *Julie, My Love* written from her husband David's perspective. His stories are filled with keen insights, humor, and transparency. Their romance, overseas experiences, and life-long commitment to each other will inspire you.

A wife of noble character who can find?
She is worth far more than rubies.
Her husband has full confidence in her
and lacks nothing of value.
She brings him good, not harm,
all the days of her life.

Proverbs 31:10-12

Donna Krstulovich, Ph.D.
Springfield, Missouri

# A WORD FROM THE AUTHOR

I penned *Julie, My Love* to honor my wife and to encourage you. When Julie became convinced stories from her life could uplift and strengthen others, she finally gave me permission to write about her. It is Julie's wish never to draw attention to herself, but to her Lord. She considers herself an ordinary person who desires to serve God with all her heart. Julie believes anyone can do the same.

As I wrote accounts from Julie's life, at times, tears of gratitude flowed as I thanked God for choosing such a beautiful jewel to be my wife.

I've selected certain stories from Julie's life that I hope will enhearten you. I've created some settings to enhance the conversations. Some names have been changed to respect and protect certain individuals.

David Leatherberry

# CONTENTS

# THE WEDDING

The organist emphatically struck the chord to announce the appearance of the bride. Everyone in the church stood, turned, and looked up the aisle anticipating her entrance. Then, there she was!

Julie walked slowly down the aisle with her stunning white wedding gown flowing around her. Her face was radiant. She was my bride. Our enraptured eyes met. Then with hands united we moved up the stairs to the altar.

Together we had designed our wedding ceremony to emphasize our lifelong commitment to each other, our intention to establish a home where our Savior would always be honored, and our love for each other would be evident to others.

As the ceremony concluded, the minister asked us to turn around to face the audience and then proudly announced, "May I introduce to you for the first time the new Mr. and Mrs. David Leatherberry!" Julie and I joyfully paraded quickly to the back of the church to greet our families and friends.

The moment we had dreamed about had become a reality. Julie, my love was now Julie, my wife!

Our wedding day was August 15, 1964. Julie was 21 years old and I was 22. Our beautiful and sacred wedding ceremony always remains etched in our minds. It was the beginning of our life's journey together. We were young, yet confident and excited about our future because we knew Christ was the center of our marriage.

# INTRIGUED

Julie Parry, a cute petite brunette entered my world in the spring of my sophomore year at Howland High School. She was the new girl in our class. This teenager was shy, pleasant and unassuming. Julie believed the Lord had spoken to her heart to begin a Youth for Christ club at Howland High. Due to her persistence, in the fall of our junior year permission was granted for our school to have a YFC club.

Julie was elected president and I was chosen vice president. Together, we often planned the activities of the club. This enabled me to become better acquainted with her. By the beginning of my senior year, Julie Parry greatly intrigued me.

Not wanting to draw attention to herself, Julie was reluctant to talk about herself. It was her habit to first think of others. In time I convinced her to tell me about herself. I learned when Julie was in third grade in Warren, Ohio, she lived in a low-income housing project. Although her father was an alcoholic, on Sunday mornings he permitted Julie and her younger brother, Tommy, to ride a church bus to a nearby store-front mission church. Joe and Jenny Stevens, founders of the church, had hearts full of compassion for children. During the week tall and energetic Joe was the local mailman. The children loved the Stevens and called them Uncle Joe and Aunt Jenny.

Julie was excited to memorize the first two Scripture verses taught to her by Aunt Jenny. They were John

3:16, "For God so loved the world, that he gave his only begotten Son, that whosoever believeth in him should not perish, but have everlasting life," and Acts 16:31, "And they said, 'Believe on the Lord Jesus Christ, and thou shalt be saved, and thy house'."*

Aunt Jenny shared with the children how much the Lord Jesus loved them. When she asked if they would like to give their hearts to Jesus, eight-year-old Julie responded. From then on Julie knew that Jesus loved her and was with her.

I was a curious fellow who always wanted to know the why of everything. Julie intrigued me as I especially observed her my junior year in high school. I visited Julie and her family in their home. Besides her brother, Julie had a little sister, Lucy, 12 years younger than she. They lived in a made-over garage. They seldom had hot water. A diesel stove stood in the main room and was their only source of heat during the winter, warming only that area of the house. Because of her father's drinking problem, Julie's family was dysfunctional. Often her parents fought.

What intrigued me was how Julie could be so positive and cheerful when her circumstances militated against her. I never heard her complain about her situation. Instead, she thought about others before herself. Julie respected and genuinely cared for her fellow classmates. At times I was greatly moved when I heard her sincerely pray for their spiritual well-being. It fascinated me that although many of the other girls had nicer clothes, this did not seem to disturb Julie.

I marveled at Julie's unshakeable inner security as a teenager. Her faith in the Lord Jesus Christ was

*King James Version

unmovable. Given her circumstances, I wondered how that could be at her young age.

It took me a long time to discover the secret of her strong inner security and contentment. The secret was that her heart was filled with gratitude. Julie was glad she could learn at school. She was thankful she had food and shelter. She was grateful she could serve others. It gave her great joy to know she was dearly loved by the Lord Jesus and that He was always with her. She rejoiced in the fact her sins were forgiven and the Lord was preparing a place for her in heaven. She did not take her blessings for granted.

Julie often thanked God for the wonderful, godly people He brought into her life, like Joe and Jenny Stevens. She was delighted when Joe Stevens became the director for all the high school Youth for Christ clubs in our area. He enthusiastically gave direction to our Saturday night YFC rallies. He constantly encouraged Julie and gave her wise advice as she led our Howland YFC club.

Julie often thanked God for Rev. William Uncapher who had become her pastor when she was nine years old. Rev. Uncapher had been a hard-boiled, cursing steamroller operator at the Republic Steel Plant in Warren. Then in his mid-thirties, the Lord Jesus transformed his life and called him into the ministry. He self-studied and began a church with a few people. Rev. Uncapher and his devout wife Miriam took Julie under their wings and enabled her to grow in the Lord. She usually spent Sunday afternoons in their home with them and their two daughters who were near her age.

# PRAYING FOR THE GIRL I WOULD MARRY

When I was 13 years old and in the seventh grade, every Sunday afternoon I propped myself up on my bed in my small attic-like bedroom and turned on the radio. First I listened to Dr. Hoffmann on the Lutheran Hour followed by Billy Graham on the Hour of Decision. I tried to soak in everything these men of God said.

One afternoon Billy Graham stated that as a youth, you should start praying for the person you will marry. I thought, *That's a good idea.* I wondered what the girl I'd marry looked like. I wondered where she lived and what she was doing. I knew her Christian character would be outstanding. For you see, I had already decided that was the only kind of girl I'd marry.

Although no one ever told me I should have private devotions, for some unknown reason the thought occurred to me that it would be a good idea to read a chapter from the Bible daily and pray. It also came to my mind that I should keep in my Bible a list of the people I should pray for each day. After hearing Rev. Graham's advice, I added to my prayer list the girl I would marry. I began praying such prayers as this: "God, wherever she is, bless her and keep her safe today. Please keep her just for me. Please help her to overcome any difficulties and help her to grow in You."

I wondered when and where I would meet her. And how I would know she was the girl for me. But I was sure, in time, I would know.

Thank you, Billy Graham, for the great idea you
gave me.

*Howland, Ohio 1959*

## OUR FIRST "DATE"

By the time we were seniors at Howland High, Julie
and I had become good friends. I admired and
respected her. But for some unknown reason, I did not
think of her romantically. We were just good friends.

Late that fall my church's youth group scheduled
a hayride. You could invite a date. I liked the idea. I
kept trying to decide which girl I should invite. Finally,
I decided on a young lady whose company I thought
I would enjoy. I told Julie about the hayride and the
young lady I planned to invite. Julie responded, "That's
wonderful, David. She is a lovely person."

But when I invited the young lady, she declined.
I could not understand why. I told Julie about the
refusal and that now I had another girl in mind. When
I told Julie who she was, Julie said, "David, that's a very
good choice." So I happily got up the courage to ask
the good choice. I tried not to show my embarrassment
when Good Choice gave me a weak excuse why she
couldn't accept my gracious invitation. My ego was
beginning to take a real beating.

I told Julie about my latest rejection and said, "But
I have a good idea. There is a girl I had a big crush on
when I was in the third grade in Bristolville. I always

liked her. I think I will drive over to Bristolville, find her, and ask her to go on the hayride with me." Julie responded, "David, that's a great idea." So I drove to Bristolville, located Eva Jean's house, and bravely knocked on the front door. Eva opened the door and was very surprised to see me. I had to remind her who I was, but then she remembered me. She politely refused my cordial invitation and said she was going steady with another guy.

It was a sad drive back to Howland. The next evening, I drove down the hill to Julie's place. We sat together on her front porch swing. "Well, David, how did it go?" she asked with a smile.

"Not so good," I replied. "Eva Jean has a steady boyfriend. She politely refused my invitation."

"Sorry to hear that."

I sat there quietly for a while, pondering my problem. The next night was the hayride and I still had no date.

"Julie," I said, "would you like to go with me tomorrow night on the hayride?"

Without a moment's hesitation she replied, "Sure, David, why not?"

"Thanks, Julie," I said with a smile of relief. She had just solved my problem. As I got up from the porch swing I said, "I'll pick you up tomorrow evening at 5:30."

"Sounds good!" Julie cheerfully replied.

As I drove home I thought, *This girl is amazing.* How incredible that she was not upset with me. Most girls would have said, "Bye, bye, buddy, you are on your own," instead of helping me to save face.

My friend Julie and I had a very enjoyable time together with the other young people as the farmer drove the tractor and pulled the hay wagon. After the ride we enjoyed singing and roasting wieners and marshmallows around the campfire. Our youth leader shared a heartwarming devotional from the Bible.

I believe Julie and I had such a delightful time because we were just friends and were not trying to impress each other. After I dropped her off at her house and drove home, I thought, what a remarkable girl she is. Perhaps I need to spend more time with her. It also dawned on me that God had answered my prayer that I would take the right girl on the hayride. I had, indeed!

## MAKING A HARD DECISION

During my senior year I found ways to spend more time with Julie. When spring came, we often sat on her porch swing just talking. I am a talkative person and Julie is a good listener. Often I talked about my dreams for the future. I was a big dreamer because I believed the book of Acts in the Bible is normative for today, therefore God can still do the impossible. Most people would have thought I was just an idealistic teenager who someday would face reality. But Julie was the one person who took very seriously what I said. At times she would nod her head and say *uh huh* as I dreamed out loud.

I started to realize how much I liked this girl and how easy it would be to fall in love with Julie. I decided

I needed to guard my heart, because I knew at age 14 God had clearly called me into the ministry. That meant much preparation. Although I was beginning to feel quite mature, I couldn't allow myself to become serious with Julie.

Soon the time arrived for Julie and me to graduate from Howland High School. Youth for Christ had a special graduation banquet for the seniors in our area. Of course I planned to take Julie to the celebration. I became even more concerned that if I were not careful, I really could fall in love with Julie the summer after graduation. In order to guard my heart, I decided I could not see Julie all summer even though she lived only a mile and a half from me. This was a difficult decision to make. A few days before the banquet I visited with her. I explained why I could not see her during the coming summer. She listened intently and softly responded, "I understand, David." I knew she did. She had come to believe in me and wanted the best for my life. And she knew I wanted the best for hers.

After a joyful time at the YFC graduation banquet, I quietly drove Julie home. We lingered on her front porch swing. Before I left, we reverently bowed our heads and prayed.

It was a great challenge to keep my commitment not to see Julie all summer. Every day on the way to work I had to drive by her house. But I knew it was right for me not to risk short-circuiting God's plan for my life.

The first day of September, I went to see Julie to say goodbye just before she went east to Nyack College*

*Now—Alliance University

in New York. Soon I would travel west to enroll in
Evangel College* in Missouri. Once again, we sat on
her porch swing and enjoyed a pleasant talk.

Rev. Uncapher had encouraged Julie to take a step
of faith and believe that God would make a way for her
to enroll as a student at Nyack College. Rev. Uncapher
would drive her and his two daughters to Nyack.

I shared with Julie how God had provided a door-
to-door Fuller Brush salesman job for me. It was a
commission-only type of job. God had helped me earn
enough money to pay for my first semester. My father
was unemployed and unable to financially assist me
with college.

We talked about how God had taken care of us and
would continue to do so as we trusted Him. After a
heartwarming visit, we finally had to say goodbye. Before
we said our goodbyes, although we knew we thought
the world of each other, we talked and understood we
were not in any way committed to each other. Together
we prayed that God's will would be done in our lives.
If, in the future, we were meant for each other, He
would bring that about. As I drove home, I once again
marveled at this girl named Julie. How she so calmly
handled this situation and others constantly amazed me.
I knew her calmness and contentment flowed from her
close walk with the Lord Jesus Christ. It was good to
know God was truly first in our lives and we could fully
trust Him with our futures.

*Now—Evangel University

*New York 1960*

# GENEROUS JULIE

With only $100 in her pocket, Julie traveled by faith to Nyack College in New York. She believed God would provide a job so she could work her way through college. Julie needed the $100 as her down payment to enter Nyack. After that she would have to make monthly payments.

Sure enough, Julie was soon hired by a bakery for $1.25 an hour. She attended classes in the morning and worked 30 hours a week at the bakery. The owners, Frank and Louise, were glad to employ Julie because the students at Nyack College had an excellent reputation as honest, hard workers.

The summer after her freshman year Julie was invited to live with Frank, Louise and their curly-haired teenage daughter, nicknamed Fuzzy. Even living with another family, Julie had to carefully plan her limited budget. One day Frank watched Julie divide the funds from her salary and place each amount in a labeled envelope. One of the envelopes was marked *tithe*.

Frank asked, "What does tithe mean? What is it for?"

Julie explained, "The Bible teaches we should give the first 10% of our income to the Lord. I do that by giving it to my local church. That's my tithe."

"What!" Frank exclaimed, "Are you kidding me?! God does not expect that of you when you are trying to work your way through college!"

Julie smiled, "Oh yes, He does, Frank. God has to be first in all areas of my life. I lose out when I do not joyfully obey Him. He knows what is best for my life. He takes good care of me. Frank, you and Louise hired me, didn't you? When I needed a job, He provided it through you."

Frank just shook his head and walked away not convinced, but in his heart, he admired Julie.

Julie had worked her way through high school by working in a candy store. She gave her tithe from the very first dollar she earned and has done so ever since.

As Julie and I got to know each other, I was pleased to realize tithing was very important to both of us. I shared with Julie the story of when I was ten years old and made my first dollar by helping a new neighbor clean out her cellar. When my dad came home from his factory job, I proudly showed him my dollar. He sat me down and explained that the first 10% of that dollar belonged to God. Anything more was an offering to God. The next Sunday I joyfully put my dime in the offering plate as well as another nickel, because I wanted to also give an offering to God. From that day forward I have always first given my tithe from all income.

United in our firm belief regarding tithing was a beautiful foundation stone for our marriage. After our first year of marriage, Julie and I lived in a mobile home (called a trailer in those days) in Fort Lee, New Jersey, near the George Washington Bridge that crossed into New York City. I was in graduate school in New York City. Julie was hired as a first-grade teacher at a private Jewish school. It's amazing that they hired her since she was still working toward her undergraduate degree. Without a degree, she was, of course, given a lower salary. We lived on a financial shoestring, but it was God's financial shoestring! We always had enough pennies in our penny jar to pay for my bus fare into New York City. And we felt blessed that a man in the neighborhood sold dented cans of food for half price.

People often ask Julie and me the secret to our happy marriage. One of those secrets is our delight in giving beyond our tithe to facilitate another person in need as well as giving to a worthy cause for Christ. This brings overflowing joy to our hearts.

Julie has said to me more than once, "Oh, David, isn't it marvelous that our Heavenly Father enables us to give!" Indeed, it is. The words of Jesus, "It is more blessed to give than to receive," are so very true.

*Howland, Ohio 1962*

# AWKWARD OBEDIENCE

From an early age, I had promised myself I would never tell a girl I loved her unless she was the girl I wanted to marry. I finally came to the conclusion Julie was that girl. It was now the end of the summer after my sophomore year at Evangel College. After working all summer in New York, Julie had just arrived home to see her family. I was excited to see her.

Late one afternoon as I drove to her house, I decided the time had come to tell Julie I loved her. I could not think of one reason why I shouldn't. But on the way the Holy Spirit spoke to my heart that this was not the day to tell her. This was one time I did not want to hear His voice. I rationalized it was just me making up such a thought. After all, I said to myself, I can't think of one reason why I should not tell Julie I love her.

It was so delightful to see Julie and to sit with her once again on the front porch swing. Finally, I looked at her with my best smile and said, "Julie, I love you." The moment I uttered those words, I suddenly became sick. I couldn't talk. I got up from the swing without a word to Julie, got into my dad's old Studebaker, and drove home. I immediately went upstairs to my attic-like bedroom and got down on my knees. I felt a million miles away from God. I knew I had directly disobeyed Him. I deeply repented.

The next morning I again drove the mile and a half to Julie's house. I knocked on the door. She opened the door and smiled. Red-faced, I awkwardly said, "Julie, I am sorry, but I have to take back what I said yesterday."

At that point, I hoped the ground would open and I would disappear. Instead of slamming the door in my face, which I deserved, she paused for a moment, and then gave me an understanding look. "That's alright, David, we got a little ahead of ourselves yesterday. We need to give things time."

Then she sweetly smiled. I just nodded. I could not speak. My embarrassment overwhelmed me. Finally I forced a smile and said, "Thanks, Julie." I left with Julie still standing in the doorway.

As I drove a little ways north on Route 46 before turning right and going up the hill on Howland Springs Road, my heart was crushed, for I truly loved Julie. Her response caused me to love her all the more. It mystified me how this girl could feel so secure that she could think about my feelings before her own. "Oh God," I cried out as I drove, "I sure got myself in a mess. What am I to do now?"

I returned to Evangel College for my junior year. I believed Julie was the girl for me, but I had to be sure she was God's choice. Three different times that fall I earnestly knelt in the prayer chapel, seeking the Lord regarding Julie. He assured me she was His choice. I could not wait until Christmas to see her.

*Ohio 1962*

## WILL YOU MARRY ME?

Christmas vacation arrived in our junior year of college. Spending time with Julie flooded my heart with joy.

On New Year's Eve, we visited a close friend. While driving Julie home through falling snow, I told Julie I loved her and the many reasons why. When we arrived at her house we sat in the car and talked. Then looking into her sparkling, beautiful brown eyes, I said, "Julie, will you marry me?"

Gently she answered, "David, I would like to say yes, because I dearly love you too, but first I must pray and make sure it's God's will."

Her answer made me admire her even more. This was the kind of girl I wanted to marry.

Six weeks later, Julie said *yes*. We set our wedding date for August 15 of the next year, the summer after I would graduate from Evangel.

*Ohio 1963*

## "YOU WHAT?!"

I walked briskly down my dorm hallway to the pay phone. I was excited to call my mother in Ohio, 800 miles away. It was spring near the end of my junior year at Evangel College. Julie and I became engaged the previous February, but due to Julie's circumstances at home, we did not tell anyone. Now I felt it was time to tell my mother.

I dropped the correct number of coins into the pay telephone and dialed the number. Mom answered.

"Hello, Mom, this is David."

"Well, hello, David. This is a pleasant surprise. How are you?"

"I'm fine. Mom, I have some tremendous news! I plan to marry Julie in August. She is definitely the right girl for me."

"You what?!"

"I'm going to marry Julie."

Suddenly my mother's voice became loud. "You can't do that! You have another year of college to complete!" I thought Mom was going to come through the telephone wire. I was surprised since my mother was not the excitable type. I knew Mom desired the best for me, but she did not want me to mess things up before I graduated.

"Please calm down, Mom. I don't mean this August. I mean a year from this August."

"Oh, okay, David, that's different," she responded in her normal tone of voice.

Mom listened carefully as I shared why I believed Julie was God's choice for me.

After we hung up Mom immediately telephoned my Aunt Frances. "Frances, I just talked with David. He plans to marry Julie Parry. I need to come over right away so we can pray about this."

"Bea, come right now and we will seek the Lord." Aunt Frances was Mom's closest prayer partner and they often prayed together.

Although Mom believed I knew how to hear from the Lord, when it came to her son's marriage she had to hear from God Himself that I was marrying the right girl. After all, not only had she prayed from the day I was born that I would be a true man of God, she had also prayed for the girl I would marry. She was very fond of Julie, but now she needed to definitely know God had chosen Julie for her son.

As usual, Aunt Frances and Mom got down on their knees and poured out their hearts to God. After a while Mom sensed this word from the Lord, "My sheep know my voice and will follow me." That confirmed to Mom that Julie and I had heard from the Lord and He had chosen us for each other.

The next day Mom went to visit Julie at her house. After two and a half years at Nyack, Julie had returned

home to care for her very seriously ill mother. With great
joy Mom said, "Julie, I am delighted that God has chosen
you to be David's wife. I will be very blessed to have you as
my daughter-in-law." Julie beamed with Mom's approval.
She highly respected my mother as a godly woman.

It came to be that Mom loved Julie so much that
you would have thought Julie was her daughter and
I was the son-in-law. In fact, if at any time my mom
had thought I mistreated Julie in any way, I would have
been in deep trouble with my mother.

Once I teasingly asked my mother, "Mom, why do
you always take Julie's side and never take mine?"

Without a moment's hesitation, Mom quipped,
"Son, it is because I always like to be right!"

*Ohio 1963*

# THINKING GIRL

It was the summer between my junior and senior
college years. Julie and I were engaged. One of the
many things I loved about Julie was that she was a
thinking girl. We were able to have insightful, intellectual
discussions. I believed that was vital to our relationship.

Jesus said, "Love the Lord your God with all your
heart and with all your soul and with all your mind
and with all your strength" (Mark 12:30). The apostle
Peter wrote, "Always be prepared to give an answer to
everyone who asks you the reason for the hope that
you have" (I Peter 3:15). I believe God expects us to

use our minds. During my sophomore year of college, I had been intellectually challenged by a brilliant agnostic in my dorm. I realized that I needed to know why I believed what I believed.

One warm summer Saturday afternoon, Julie and I sat on a picnic blanket at the south end of Mosquito Lake. I read to Julie from the Christian apologetic book, *Therefore Stand* by Wilbur M. Smith. I had thoroughly studied this 614-page classic and enthusiastically shared with Julie the insights I had gained.

After reading a section of the book I asked, "Julie, what do you think?"

Julie thought for a moment, "David, that certainly stimulates a person's thinking. And as you have been saying, it's crucial that we know why we believe what we believe and are able to give the objective basis for our faith."

We spent the afternoon reading and discussing Wilbur Smith's masterpiece. After I dropped Julie off at her home, I thought to myself, *This girl is not only beautiful and sweet, but she's also a real thinker.* This confirmed once again that God had chosen the right girl for me.

*Summer 1964*

# THE MYSTERY OF LOVE

I sat down in a rickety old lawn chair under the grape arbor in the backyard of my parents' home at 330 Huntley Drive in Howland, Ohio. The name of the road sounded high-class, but the unpaved road told the

truth. It was a hot, sticky day in June. I had graduated
from college in May and was fortunate to have a
summer job at the Grinnell factory in Warren.

I had just returned from work and sat with a cold
Coca-Cola in my hand. My mother was busy preparing
the evening meal. I looked across our green lawn
and saw a big gray rabbit enjoying an early dinner,
munching on the grass near the tree line at the end of
our property. I always enjoyed observing wildlife.

My thoughts turned to the girl with whom I had
so deeply fallen in love. We were to be married in
August. I wondered how I could be so blessed to have
won her heart. She was beyond my greatest dreams.
I asked myself the question, *"How did it come about that I
fell in love with Julie and know she is the one and only for me?"*

Of course, I reminisced about the time when I was
13 and started to pray for the girl I would marry. I
remembered how Julie intrigued me in high school.
I remembered how disciplined I had been to not go
see her all summer after graduation from high school.
I reflected on the time we chose not to commit
ourselves to each other, but prayed together that
God's will would be done in our lives. It came to my
mind how three different times in the college chapel I
earnestly sought God, wanting to be sure Julie was the
girl He had chosen for me. He assured me she was.

But as I sat there pondering, I still wondered
about the mystery of being so deeply in love with Julie.
I loved her as I loved no one else. It was deeper than
any love I had ever experienced outside of my love for
Christ. It ran far deeper than my emotions, greater than

my attraction to her physical beauty and her shy, radiant personality. I could not explain this love I had for her, wanting her to be my wife forever. I had never before experienced such a profound love.

I gazed into the beautiful blue sky dotted with fluffy white clouds and spoke to God, "Lord, my heart is overflowing with love for Julie. It is a mystery to me how incredible this can be. I thank you, Heavenly Father, for the beautiful work of love you have done in our hearts for each other. What a sacred gift it is. I shall be forever thankful." I sat quietly for a while enjoying the presence of the Lord. It seemed to me I could almost see Him smiling.

## The Visit with Aunt Lois

One day I stopped by after work just to chat with my Aunt Lois. It did occur to me that she might have an extra piece of apple pie on hand. Aunt Lois constantly radiated joy and always seemed delighted to see me.

"Well, hello Davey," she cheerfully greeted me as she opened the screen door. "Come on in. This is a pleasant surprise. What brings you by?"

"Oh, Aunt Lois, you know I love to hang out with you when I can."

She smiled. "Of course I am sure it has nothing to do with the apple pies I bake."

Aunt Lois continued, "I just happen to have baked a fresh apple pie today. If you don't think it will spoil your supper, I'll serve you a piece."

"I can assure you it will not spoil my supper. Besides, Aunt Lois, I mustn't be rude and refuse such a kind offer." We both laughed as we headed for the kitchen.

We sat at the twice-painted small white table as I fulfilled my social obligation by devouring the large piece of pie placed before me, along with a cold glass of milk. Aunt Lois drank a warm cup of coffee.

"Davey, how many days before you marry that dream girl of yours?" she asked with a big grin.

"Exactly 60 days until I marry the most incredible girl in the world!"

"Julie is a precious jewel, that's for sure. Nephew, you are very blessed indeed."

"I know."

Aunt Lois chuckled, "Why Davey, you look very starry-eyed."

I blushed.

"Davey, may I make a few suggestions about how you should work at your marriage to keep it beautiful? You see, when a garden is freshly tilled and planted with corn, beans, tomatoes, cucumbers, lettuce, carrots, etc., it looks beautiful and it is. But to keep it beautiful, it must be cultivated and constantly weeded. It's the same way with marriage. Davey, your love will fade in time if you and Julie don't intentionally cultivate and keep it weeded."

I was quiet for a moment pondering her words. "Please, Aunt Lois, share with me your suggestions. I'm ready to listen." So, point by point, she carefully articulated her words of wisdom.

Now, two days later, I sat in my backyard and carefully reflected on Aunt Lois's wise advice. I was eager to share those insights with Julie during a picnic we planned for the following weekend.

## Picnic at Mosquito Lake

The following Saturday, driving my dad's old Studebaker, I arrived with Julie at Mosquito Lake Park near the south end. The name Mosquito Lake caused me to grin. I wondered if the mosquitoes who made people's lives so miserable were proud to have received such distinct recognition. I hoped they were not out in force today.

After parking Old Reliable, we walked to a picnic table among the tall trees near the water's edge. We carefully spread the checkered tablecloth over the table. Julie unpacked the picnic basket, setting out cold chicken, potato salad, chips, cucumbers, cookies, fresh lemonade, and other tasty-looking food including fresh-cut pieces of mouth-watering watermelon. We sat down and reached across the table to hold hands as I gave thanks to the Lord.

I was delighted to spend the day with Julie. Her winsome smile always warmed my heart. I marveled at her ability to have a humble, tender heart while also displaying self-confidence without a tinge of arrogance. Her clear brown eyes reflected pure innocence.

"Julie," I said, "I had a remarkable visit with my Aunt Lois this week. She gave me good advice on how we can work at our marriage to keep it beautiful."

"David, that's thoughtful. Please tell me about it."

"Of course, she said we should always keep Christ at the center of our marriage by praying together each day. She said sometimes we may become upset with each other. At such times we should probably wait to cool down before we pray. We may need to give each other some space."

Julie teased, "Why, David, I cannot imagine us getting upset with each other."

I laughed. "Being human, there's a good possibility it will happen. Even though I know you are almost perfect!"

Julie smiled and responded, "But you know, David, it seems to me if we pray together each day it will reduce the number of disagreements. And it will be harder to stay upset when we kneel together before our Lord. What else did Aunt Lois say?"

"She said we need to be ready to forgive each other, and be willing to ask for forgiveness. May I add, Sweetheart, I believe I should be the first to ask for forgiveness since I will be the head of our household."

"Sounds like wisdom to me." Julie smiled.

"Julie, I never want to take you for granted. I have seen marriages start out well but after five years the husband and wife take each other for granted. This causes a marriage to erode."

"David, I hear you. We cannot let that happen."

"Sweetheart, I have an idea. Let's promise each other that every day we will verbally tell each other *I love you*. I never want us to ever become presumptuous about our love for each other."

"I wholeheartedly agree."

"You know, Julie, according to psychological studies our marriage is not likely to be successful since we come from dysfunctional homes, due to your father being an alcoholic and my father's self-absorbing emotional problems."

Julie responded, "That means we must be aware that unexpected difficulties can arise. We can't allow them to throw us. If we run into a problem we can't handle, we should be humble enough to seek outside help from someone like your Aunt Lois or a good Christian counselor."

"Sweetheart, that's a good point. You know what else my Aunt Lois said? She said we should be careful not to criticize each other's family or relatives because we are far more emotionally attached to our family members than we realize. We can hurt each other if we are not wise about this. It doesn't mean we shut our eyes to the weaknesses they may have, but we don't need to dwell on them."

"Hmmm, that's perceptive," Julie thoughtfully responded.

I began to laugh.

"David, what in the world are you laughing about?"

"Sweetheart, forgive me, but I just had a funny memory about when I was in elementary school. Sometimes when the kids got upset with each other, they would shout, 'Your mother wears combat boots.' That was the worst insult they could think of. At times I was tempted to say the same thing to another kid, but I resisted because I knew Jesus wouldn't be pleased. Besides, I had no desire to experience my mother's discipline if she found out I said anything like that."

We both laughed.

"Julie, do any of your family members wear combat boots?'

Julie picked up a glass of water and threw the water on me. "David, you can be sure I'll never tell you if they do!"

Wiping my face with a couple of paper towels, I laughed so hard tears came to my eyes. *Yes, sir, this girl has spunk. That's another reason I love her so much.*

"Julie, have you ever heard a husband or wife criticize each other in front of other people?"

"Yes, sorry to say."

"So have I."

"Aunt Lois stressed how very hurtful that is. Let's agree we won't do that."

"David, I agree."

"Amen, and let's not criticize each other, even as a joke. That can cut deep in a backhanded way."

"What other insights did Aunt Lois mention?"

"Well, she said when we have to make an important decision and one of us persuades the other to agree to go his or her way, and then it doesn't work out, we are not permitted to say, 'I told you so!'"

Julie laughed. "At times that may be a hard principle to keep, but I believe we can. That's quite insightful."

I started to laugh again. "Julie, my love, Aunt Lois stressed that we would need to know how to fight fair."

"Fight?! Fight fair!" Julie exclaimed! "Why, David, I can't imagine us ever fighting! Can you?!"

I grinned. "Of course not! But I still want to know, does your mother wear combat boots?"

I felt a swift kick to my shin under the table. "No, but I do! And what are you going to do about it?"

"Okay, okay, but be sure you fight fair!"

Julie sprang up from the table, looked me straight in the eye, and shouted quietly, "You're the one I am worried about not fighting fair."

We roared with laughter as Julie mockingly raised her fists.

Then she sat down again. "Okay, David, tell me how we can fight fair and I'll see if I agree."

I smiled big and thought about how I loved this shy girl who could be so feisty. "Aunt Lois says we should keep our emotions under control, patiently listen to each other, and not be thinking about what we are going to say next. We'll need to try to place ourselves in each other's shoes. We'll need to stick with the relevant issue at hand and not bring up things from the past or other unrelated issues. We have to be willing to compromise. Also, she said sometimes when you are in the middle of a good fair fight, the best solution is simply to agree to disagree."

I began chuckling and added, "And Sweetheart, Aunt Lois said the best thing about a vigorous fair fight is making up afterwards." Julie blushed.

She reached into her red purse and pulled out a small notebook and pen. "I think we should write all these principles down and put them into practice from the very beginning of our marriage."

So again we reviewed Aunt Lois's words of wisdom. Julie wrote them down one by one. After she finished writing, she looked up and smiled sweetly. "We will call these Aunt Lois's Commandments and hang them on the walls of our hearts." And so we did.

Now, 58 years later, those commandments are still hanging on the walls of our hearts. Due to the grace of God, we are still practicing them. Our *garden* has stayed cultivated, weeded, and beautiful. Thank you, Aunt Lois.

# AN OVERFLOW OF THE HOLY SPIRIT

In February, 1965, Julie and I were schoolteachers in Mineral Ridge and Leavittsburg, Ohio. We had been married six months when we were invited to attend a charismatic conference at a hotel in Washington, D.C. Hundreds of people were in attendance. They came to hear the testimonies of many businessmen and others who had received the baptism of the Holy Spirit with the evidence of speaking in tongues. Most came desiring to receive their own Pentecostal experience as described in the book of Acts.

Julie and I were amazed that those in attendance were from many different church denominations: Lutheran, Methodist, Baptist, Presbyterian, Mennonite, Episcopalian, etc.

One evening the speaker invited those who desired to receive the Holy Spirit baptism to please go to another designated room where Harald Bredesen would lead the prayer time.

Dozens of people left their seats in the main conference room and headed for the prayer room.

Julie joined them. I remained seated. The year before we were married, after weeks of earnestly seeking the Lord, I was wonderfully renewed in the Holy Spirit and now often prayed in a supernatural prayer language. Of course I had shared that experience with Julie. She thought it was biblical but had thoughtful questions.

I greatly admired Julie's practice to carefully examine what Scripture says on any subject. So she decided to study Scripture about the baptism in the Holy Spirit. In time she came to these conclusions: speaking in tongues empowers your witnessing; it builds you up in God; it enables you to pray when you do not know how to pray about a matter; it increases your intimacy with God; it helps you to be more sensitive to the voice of the Holy Spirit; it enhances your worship of God.

Julie also concluded that since the Apostle Paul constantly prayed in tongues and wished that others would do the same, it must be very important. But why did Paul write, "Do all speak in tongues?" At first she thought Paul meant speaking in tongues was not for everybody. Then she realized he was referring to a person giving a message in tongues in public and a different person giving the interpretation of that message. This is different from devotional tongues one receives when baptized in the Holy Spirit. This does not mean the baptism in the Holy Spirit is limited to certain persons but is available to anyone. Consequently, Julie decided the Holy Spirit baptism with speaking in tongues was accessible to her.* She began to earnestly seek for the baptism in the Holy Spirit. Therefore, at the conference she responded to the invitation.

*Acts 1:8; I Corinthians 12:10,30; I Corinthians 14:5, 13-18

Later she returned to the main conference room. With tears flowing down her cheeks, she whispered what happened. Others had quietly prayed for her and she began to pray in a supernatural prayer language. It was an overflow of the Holy Spirit she had received when she was born again at age eight.

That night when we returned to our hotel room full of joy, the Holy Spirit moved upon us in a special way as we both prayed in a supernatural prayer language. We experienced deep spiritual unity. Since that day, often together, we praise our Savior and intercede for others in tongues.

# CALLED

In 1967, Julie and I moved to the Chicago area so I could attend Trinity Evangelical Divinity School in Deerfield, Illinois, to prepare for the ministry. Julie was hired as a first-grade teacher.

Monday, February 12, 1968, began as a very ordinary day. However, it proved to be a day that would drastically change our lives. Since Julie had the day off from teaching, I asked, "Why don't you come to class with me?"

"Good idea," she responded, happy not to spend a rainy, dreary day alone in our little apartment—even though it was elegantly furnished with $70 worth of contemporary Goodwill and modern Salvation Army.

Trinity had a daily chapel service which we attended. The speaker was a missionary who ministered in a

South American country. The redheaded middle-aged man made a fiery presentation.

At the close of his 20-minute message, the speaker concluded, "Every born-again believer should get down on his or her knees and tell the Lord Jesus Christ he is available to serve Him on foreign soil."

Those words arrested my attention.

The missionary continued, "If God doesn't call you, you are no less spiritual." Relief flooded me as I thought, *Oh, good, because I'm trying to follow the Lord with all my heart.*

I could not conceive of going overseas, especially if it necessitated learning another language. But the speaker's words would not leave my mind.

*Every believer,* I thought. *How interesting. I've never asked God if I should go or not.*

That evening in our little apartment I asked Julie, "How can we be followers of Christ if we aren't willing to do absolutely anything He asks?"

She shrugged as if she knew the answer but was carefully considering the implications while letting me think about it.

The following morning, we knelt together by the couch, and I prayed, "Lord, Julie and I want you to know this morning that we are available to serve anywhere in the world for You."

After honestly speaking that to the Lord, the availability issue was settled. We never expected anything more to come of it. In fact, I thought the whole matter was finished. But over the next few weeks I got the feeling that maybe, just maybe, God was calling Julie and me to serve Him overseas.

A friend gave Julie the book *Hudson Taylor and Maria, Pioneers to China* by John Pollock, and told her, "You just have to read this book." We decided to read it together each night. Julie and I were astounded at the Taylors' love and sacrifice for the Chinese people. The more we read, the more we realized that the supreme, voluntary sacrifice of Christ for our sins was the motivating factor behind Hudson and Maria's compassion. Deep in our hearts we realized the couple did not just intellectually accept the fact of Christ's sacrifice on the cross; they were fully consumed by it. They clearly saw in the sacrifice of Christ, God's own self-giving, compassionate love for people. The Taylors believed the only way to express their gratitude to God was to carry that love to others.

*Shouldn't Julie and I be willing to do the same?* I thought.

After completing the last chapter of the book, we began to weep in God's presence. Love and concern washed over us in waves and we found ourselves saying, "God, will You please send us to a people with whom we can share the love You have given us?"

Julie and I had come full circle from saying *"That's impossible"* to *"We're available"* to *"Please send us."* And indeed, we believed He would do just that. But we didn't know where.

We earnestly sought the Lord over a period of several months, asking God to reveal to us to whom we should go. In answer to our prayers, God clearly called us to the Pashtuns in Afghanistan. Julie's love for the Lord Jesus and for me made it possible for us to answer His call. I shall ever be thankful.

# LUCY

Julie and I were married only four years when we had the joy of raising a teenager. In the summer of 1968 Julie's thirteen-year-old sister, Lucy, came to live with us.

Julie's alcoholic father had divorced her mother. She had suffered a stroke that left her partially paralyzed and unable to care for Lucy. We were given legal custody. Julie's Aunt Lola and her husband, Armand, cared for Julie's mother.

When Lucy came to us we lived in Evanston, Illinois, where Julie taught first graders at Roycemore, a prestigious private school. Because Julie taught there, Lucy could attend free of charge. Most of the girls came from wealthy families. Since the school required students to wear uniforms, it was easier for Lucy to fit in. At this time I was attending Trinity Evangelical Divinity School in Deerfield, Illinois.

Lucy chose to follow the example of her sister in following the Lord Jesus Christ. They were great friends. Julie understood her sister, always had time for her, and knew how to guide her patiently and wisely. Sometimes Lucy would test my patience. At times she was not as diplomatic with me as Julie was, but we dearly loved each other.

Lucy entered her senior year at Evangel College the same year Julie and I first left to serve overseas. She graduated and became an excellent elementary school teacher. Unfortunately, she developed a severe case of rheumatoid arthritis that caused constant pain. Finally, it crippled her so badly that she could no longer teach. Life seemed so unfair. Julie had perfect health while Lucy's health was just the opposite. Yet we never heard Lucy complain to the Lord because she was not healed. Instead, she trusted and praised Him and often prayed for us.

The day came when God called Lucy home, January 22, 2011. It was 2:00 a.m. in a nursing home in Springfield, Missouri. Julie and I sat quietly near the bedside of our beloved Lucy. At 57 years of age, she was about to enter heaven. Our hearts were heavy at the thought of her no longer being with us.

Our close friend, Joshua Payne, who had been our personal assistant in Russia, stood by her bedside. Softly and slowly he spoke to Lucy. He knew that although she could not speak, she could hear him. "Lucy, I want to thank you for the joy you have brought to David and Julie. You know how much they love you. And they know how much you love them. They are right here by you. Thank you for the special blessing you have been to them. Lucy, it's okay now to leave for heaven. Jesus is waiting there to receive you. You don't have to stay here any longer. David and Julie will be joining you later. Thank you for being a loving sister to Julie and a special friend to David."

Julie and I felt the Presence of the Lord as Lucy went home. Tears, mingled with sorrow, joy, and peace, slipped from our eyes. Lucy would no longer suffer as she had for so many years. I held Julie in my arms as she wept on my shoulder.

Julie and I dearly loved Lucy and greatly miss her. I am grateful to Julie who modeled for her sister the Christlike way to live.

▲ Julie in elementary school.

◀ Joyous Julie.

▲ David and Julie cutting their wedding cake. Delightfully in love.

▲ Julie's sister Lucy.

David and Julie in their
daily national dress. ▶

▲ Julie's good friend, an Afghan Pashtun war widow.

▲ *The Afghan children, neighbors in Kandahar, Afghanistan.*

▲ *David and Julie, 1990.*

▲ *Julie (on the left) with Yazidi women in Kurdistan, Iraq.*

▲ *Julie with a daughter of a Yazidi war widow.*

*1975*

# BEFORE THE COMMITTEE

In six weeks, Julie and I would appear before the Executive Committee of the Assemblies of God, Division of Foreign Missions* in Springfield, Missouri. Before the interview, we would undergo three days of extensive testing. One of the tests required us within one hour to answer 150 questions taken from any place in the Bible. For seven years we had anticipated this momentous day. This committee would approve or disapprove our appointment as missionaries.

"Julie," I admitted as we sat across from each other at our kitchen table, "the test of 150 questions from anywhere in the whole Bible really scares me."

Julie smiled. "David, you will do just fine. Don't worry."

"But, Julie, I am worried. I must start studying now!"

For the next six weeks I studied the Bible every possible moment. I carefully read survey books of the Old and New Testaments and anything else I thought might be helpful.

One day I asked Julie, "Don't you think you should be studying for the Bible exam? It's not going to be an easy test. If we cannot prove we really know the Bible, the committee may doubt our call to be missionaries."

Julie responded, "Well, David, I don't have the time because I have so much to handle these days. Besides, I think I'll do okay."

*Now--Assemblies of God World Missions*

Her reply did not thrill my heart, but what could I do?

We took the tests but were not immediately given the results. Finally the day came to go before the committee who were experienced missionaries. As we entered the conference room, my mouth went dry. The committee members looked very serious. The first thing they did was read to us the results of the tests we had taken.

One of the men with a stern expression on his face asked, "David, did you and Julie sit next to each other when you took the Bible exam? It is interesting that you both scored in the 94th percentile. How do you explain that?"

Julie cheerfully piped up, "That's because I typed all of David's papers while he was in seminary."

The room erupted in laughter. These godly men were having fun putting us on. As we continued, they graciously asked us perceptive questions. They knew from experience what it took to be a successful missionary in another culture. To help candidates, they kindly pointed out any weakness that needed to be strengthened.

Julie and I will never forget the first question asked by J. Philip Hogan, the chairman of the committee, "David, you tell us you are called to be a missionary. You pioneered and pastored a church in Lansing, Illinois. Please tell us what your church has done for missions."

I was glad I could tell him our church had been a missions-minded church from its inception and all it had done for missions.

On our drive to our home near Lansing, I lamented to Julie, "Honey, life is so unfair. I studied hard day and night for six weeks preparing for the Bible exam. You didn't lift a finger to prepare."

"Sweetheart," she replied as she reached over and squeezed my hand, "I have studied the Bible since I was a little eight-year-old girl, and besides, remember it is true that I typed all your papers. The Lord knew there were a number of other important things I needed to accomplish."

A few days later we received official word that we were fully approved as missionaries. Joyful tears flowed as we hugged each other, and on our knees we thanked our Heavenly Father for the privilege He was giving us. It was one of the happiest days of our lives.

## ON THE MOUNTAIN

After our arrival in Afghanistan, August 1976, Julie and I were fully absorbed in language study our first year. However, later we were delighted to be invited to join a team of eight international friends who planned to take at least a 21-day hike in the Hindu Kush Mountain range.

The Hindu Kush is a 600-mile mountain range that flows out of the Pamir Knot to form the backbone of Afghanistan. The Pamir Knot is the region in northeast Afghanistan where Tajikistan, Pakistan, and China meet. It is called the "roof of the world" since it is an incredible collection of lofty mountain peaks, many of which rise above 20,000 feet.

The hike would give us a total change from language study, and the opportunity to see much of the beauty of northern Afghanistan. Our adventure began on August 8th. Three days later we arrived by our four-wheel-drive vehicles at a village named Fargzhamu. From there our hike on foot would begin. But first we purchased two pack donkeys to carry our gear. In addition, each team member carried a backpack of 25 to 35 pounds. After loading the donkeys, we set out on a narrow rocky path on a high mountainous trail.

During the second day the climb became quite strenuous as we climbed higher and higher. Then we realized each donkey's load was too heavy. Being without *"donkey experience"* we also had unknowingly packed their heavy loads too low on their bodies. Now on the high trail, they refused to move forward. We should have listened to the villagers who had advised us to buy three donkeys instead of two.

The only solution to the problem was to unload and leave half the load, take the other half up the trail and unload it, and then go back for the remaining half.

While the others and I worked with the donkeys, Julie said she wanted to walk on ahead. I watched as she trudged up the mountain. She was dressed in blue jeans, a long green tunic top, brown hiking boots, and a big, wide-brimmed white hat that the wind was tugging. She bobbed along confidently, finally disappearing from my view as she went over a ridge.

I had only turned for a few moments to go back down the mountain when I thought I heard Julie's voice of alarm. I cocked my head to listen. Since Julie is a self-sufficient woman who doesn't usually panic, I knew she would not call unless she was in serious trouble. I thought perhaps the wind was playing tricks on me. Yet, as I listened closely, I heard her call again.

I sprinted up the narrow trail and over the ridge to find Julie flattened against the rocky face of the mountain like putty on plate glass. She had missed the main trail. The deceptive sand and gravel path she had chosen had suddenly shifted beneath her feet. In a split second, she had plastered herself against the face of the rocky mountain far beyond my reach. She had nothing to hold on to, neither did she have a foothold. How she managed to stay in place, I do not know. I could not believe my eyes. I realized if Julie moved she would fall hundreds of feet down the mountain into the rushing river below.

"Don't move!" I said, trying to be calm and avoid frightening her more. I turned and yelled back to the others, "Come here! Hurry! Julie's in trouble!"

Tom, Ole, Betty and I grasped hands, forming a human chain. Slowly and carefully, we began to creep step by step along the face of the mountain. Tom anchored himself firmly on the main path as I edged myself painfully and slowly toward Julie. We knew at any moment we could all tumble to our deaths.

When I got close to her, Julie quietly said, "If you take my pack, then I think I can make it."

"Oh, no," I quickly responded, trying to keep panic out of my voice.

Very carefully I reached out and grasped her belt. We began inching our way back toward firm ground. A few feet from safety, somebody's foot slipped, sending sand and loose rocks tumbling and clattering down the mountain to the river.

"Don't move!" I yelled, my voice echoing off the mountain wall.

Everyone froze. When I knew for certain it was okay for us to continue, I warned, "Slowly now."

Again, we began to edge along the cold stone face of the mountain. After several agonizing steps, we finally reached safety.

I hugged Julie close and gave a huge sigh of relief. With deep gratitude, I whispered, "Thank You, God. Thank You. Thank You."

Slowly I permitted my adrenaline-charged, perspiring body to sink, trembling, to the ground. I took Julie's hand, almost afraid to let her go even though the nightmare was over. After sitting quietly by me for a few moments, tears of relief trickled down her cheeks. Concerned about the released tension, someone warned, "Watch her for shock."

"Don't worry; the Lord's near me," Julie responded. "Out there I kept calm as I thought over and over what God's Spirit had impressed upon us two nights ago, *I will be your rear guard and go before you. I will be with you.*"

Did an angel hold my angel safely on the side of the mountain? I think so.

# BLOOD FOR A NOMAD MOTHER

In December of 1979, when the Soviet Union invaded Afghanistan, Julie and I were there. We had to leave the first week of February, 1980, because our visas would not be renewed. Our hearts were broken as we boarded the green-and-white twin-prop Fokker that the Pakistan International Airlines still flew between Kabul, Afghanistan, and Peshawar, Pakistan.

After our 50-minute flight to Peshawar we went to an inexpensive but functional hotel called Jan's (pronounced John's). For the next 13 months Jan's Hotel would be our off-and-on home as we had to travel back and forth to India because we could not obtain permanent visas for Pakistan. We constantly had to reapply for short-term tourist visas.

I was grateful to God that versatile Julie always seemed to see the positive side of things instead of the negative. Sometimes she seemed unreal to me. She cheerfully washed our clothes in the sink, hung them on the rooftop of the hotel to dry and ironed them on a desktop in our little room. She did not get upset when one day someone stole the clothes. I was not a happy camper and if I could have caught the crook, I might have laid aside my sanctification for a little while. I was thankful to God that I had a wife whose happiness did not depend on circumstances or earthly possessions. She made any place a home.

One day I was wandering around in the old bazaar in Peshawar when I met a pleasant Pakistani medical student. He was doing his internship at the well-known Lady Reading Hospital. Ahmad and I became good friends. I told Ahmad that Julie and I were willing to donate blood if needed.

A few weeks later Ahmad called from the hospital with an urgent message. A nomadic Afghan refugee named

Bibigul had just given birth to a daughter and needed a blood transfusion. Since Julie had the right blood type for Bibigul, she immediately headed for the hospital.

As Julie rode in the rickshaw, anxious about the situation she would find at the hospital, she prayed earnestly for the mother and baby she had never seen, "God, I know you love Bibigul and this new little life. Help everything medically to work out right and may this blood I give be a gift of life from You."

As she prayed, the rickshaw jolted and bounced her off the seat. She almost struck her head on the roll bar. *Glad I'm shorter than David*, she thought.

Then, returning to her prayer, she said, "Lord, there are many different Pashtu dialects. Please help me to understand this woman who is likely more frightened than I am. Let me talk with ease, Lord, and help me remember the right words."

After a final bump, the rough-riding rickshaw stopped. Julie paid the driver and entered the hospital.

An hour later, Julie bolted through the door of our hotel room and skipped across the floor. Ecstatically she proclaimed, "David, mother and new baby are fine! And Bibigul and I could understand each other beautifully!"

On a subsequent visit, a thankful Bibigul asked Julie if she had any children of her own.

Julie smiled and replied, "My husband and I love children, but God has chosen not to give us a child."

Those words of explanation ended the topic, but Julie knew Bibigul felt deep sadness for her. Often in the Afghan culture a wife is considered cursed if she cannot bear a child. Also, it is shameful for a wife not to produce a son since he becomes the provider for his elderly parents.

Before she left Bibigul, Julie heard the same familiar words that had been spoken to her so often by other Muslim women. "I will pray that you will have a child."

Looking tenderly into Bibigul's eyes, Julie's response let her know she accepted Bibigul's concern. "Thank you, Bibigul. You are very kind."

## HAVING CHILDREN

Julie and I believed God would give us a child. We concluded it was His plan to do so when we were older. We love children. For seven years Julie was a first-grade teacher. She knew how to relate to children, and they loved her. I learned from Julie how to be with young children. Together we taught first, second, and third graders in Sunday school.

When later in life Julie had surgery which made it impossible for us to have a child, I was devastated. I never sobbed harder in my life than when that reality hit me. We felt we had been assured by the Lord that someday we would be parents. Therefore, because I was so crushed, it was difficult to process this reality. However, later I had an unusual experience with the Lord that healed my broken heart, an experience too sacred to share with others.

Julie amazed me. For a long time we had looked forward to being parents. She would have loved to hold

her own newborn baby in her arms. She would have
been an incredible mother. I wondered how Julie could
process this so extremely well. Perhaps one reason was
because Julie admired the attitude of Mary, the mother
of Jesus. Mary was willing to fully submit her life to
God even when at times she did not understand. Julie
desired to have the same attitude.

Once I said to Julie, "Sweetheart, I want you to
know something. You are no less a woman because you
have not given birth to a child."

Julie replied, "Thank you for saying that. I know I
am no less of a woman because I cannot have children.
I wish other women who feel so devalued or humiliated
could understand that. You have never made me feel
less because we don't have our own children. David,
thank you for loving me as I am."

Julie and I earnestly sought the Lord about whether
or not we should adopt children. He made it clear it
was His will that we should not.

*     *     *

At a later time Julie said, "You know, David, there
are a lot of Afghan women who highly respect you
because you truly love me. Do you know why they
respect you?"

"No, I don't know why."

"Because you haven't taken a second wife." Julie
was well aware that Afghan women who cannot bear
children, especially a son, often worry that due to
their barrenness, their husband will divorce them or
take a second wife. Since Julie had not had children,

such women identified with her and often shared their hearts with her.

*    *    *

Once while Julie and I were on home leave in the States, we had the privilege of attending the beautiful wedding of my remarkable cousin Brigette. Both she and her new husband, John, were dedicated followers of Jesus. I had known Brigette since she was a little girl. I had always been very proud of her.

After the wedding as we were driving from Columbus, Ohio, to our home in the Chicago area, tears began streaming down my face. For a long time I could not speak. Julie patiently waited and then asked, "Honey, what's wrong?"

Haltingly I said, "Julie, I will never have the honor of giving away my beautiful daughter as Brigette's father had. She and her father have had such a special relationship from the time she was a little child. The issue is settled with me about not having children, so why do I feel this way? I don't understand."

Julie tenderly smiled. "David, it's because you have a father's heart. That hasn't changed even though we don't have children. It's only natural that you feel this way. Honey, I am very proud that you have the passionate heart of a father."

Once again, my wife's wisdom amazed me. *How could I ever be so blessed to have Julie as my wife, God's unique gift to me?* Of course, the greatest gift anyone can receive is the gift of salvation in Christ which is available to everyone. But Julie is my unique gift from God because there is only one Julie in the whole universe. God in His mercy gave her to me.

# SINGLE WOMEN

In 1983 God performed a miracle for Julie and me. We were granted visas by the communist government in Kabul, Afghanistan, that was under the control of the Soviets. We, along with other international friends, were permitted to do hospital work. Jenny was one of those friends.

After a meaningful visit, Julie and I waved goodbye to Jenny as she drove off in her rusty old Volkswagen. We turned and entered our small house surrounded by a high mud wall and, even though the hour was late, decided to have another cup of hot green tea.

"David," Julie said after I sipped some tea, "This has been a wonderful evening. Jenny is such a remarkable person. I greatly admire her."

"So do I. Here she is from England serving God as a single lady in Kabul, Afghanistan, in an Islamic society. Being single and living here without living with your family does not fit into the cultural thinking of the Afghans. They cannot understand why her parents would give their permission to do such an outlandish thing. They presume her family doesn't care about her. They think such a single woman must be permissive."

"I know," Julie commented, "But the Christian single ladies we know have responded to the clear call of God to serve others even in Islamic countries. Their obedience to our Lord is more important to them than the circumstances. Their clean Christian living surprises the Muslims. It has caused them to stop and wonder what motivates these godly women."

"Julie, they are unique, and God uses their uniqueness. People who assume single women cannot serve in Islamic countries do not begin to understand their powerful witness for Christ. Of course, each must know they are truly called by God or, in time, the pressure of the culture could lead them to despair."

"David, just think about Jenny. She's a middle-aged dedicated nurse at the famous eye hospital here in Kabul and is also a midwife who has delivered dozens of Afghan babies born in home after home. In fact, the other day she saved the life of a baby who was born with the cord wrapped around the child's neck."

Julie continued, "I certainly enjoyed the evening with Jenny. You probably noticed that you and Jenny did most of the talking while I quietly listened. Do you know why I just listened?"

"No, Julie, I never thought about it."

"I kept quiet because single women need to share their thoughts with a man, not just other women. Often a man can give a different insightful perspective than another woman can. Single women need a brother they can trust and discuss the challenges they face. Sweetheart, you did a beautiful job tonight of thoughtfully listening to Jenny's heart as she shared some complicated issues. You helped her to carefully think things through. I'm proud of you. May we always be available to such dear servants of our Lord. And may He continue to use you in this way."

I took a deep breath as I leaned back in my chair, "Honey, I've never thought about that. Thank you for helping me to understand."

As I closed my eyes that night, I once again thanked God for the miracle of having Julie as my wife. I thought, *Julie, you are not only beautiful and feel secure in our marriage, but you're wise and keenly insightful. Yes, Julie, my love, I will love you forever.*

*Kabul 1983*

## SLAP IN THE FACE OF GOD

I sat at the kitchen table while Julie prepared our evening meal. "David, why do you look so serious? Did something happen today at work that upset you?" perceptive Julie asked.

"Well, yes," I replied. "You know how I greatly dislike confronting people, but sometimes it's necessary."

"What happened?"

"Today at the hospital I overheard Bob again teasing John about not being married. He told John he should ask the new nurse from Sweden for a date. Bob implied that John can never be a complete man until he gets married. Bob said to John, 'You are already 37 years old and beginning to bald. Time is running out on you. You better act now.'"

In dismay Julie put down her frying pan. "David, how can those who call themselves Christians, at times, be so insensitive to others?"

"Easy, Julie, we need to be careful that we keep our own attitudes right towards those who are insensitive. Remember you once said to me, 'It's vitally important we are not prejudiced against prejudiced people.'"

"You're right, Sweetheart, but it's sad that some Christians can be so thoughtless."

Julie sat down at our time-worn table.

"After John left," David continued, "I asked Bob to please step outside because I wanted to speak with him. So we walked into the walled courtyard. 'Bob', I said, 'when are you going to quit slapping God in the face?'"

"Bob looked stunned and asked, 'What are you talking about?'"

I explained, "Well, you just slapped God in the face by assuming John should be married. God does call some persons not to marry. He does that since he has a special purpose for their lives that they can only fulfill if they remain single. We all admire the great scholar John Stott because of his incredible contribution to the Body of Christ. He was called by God to remain single. When you insist that your co-worker John should marry, you are slapping God in the face by countering God's will for his life. And Bob, the Bible does not teach a single person is not complete if he or she does not marry. That's a man-made idea. A person is complete when he or she is in Christ."

"Bob listened silently to all I had to say. He admitted he had never thought about it that way. To my surprise and his great credit, he thanked me. He said he is going to apologize to John the next time he talks to him."

"Wow!" Julie exclaimed. "That was courageous of you to confront Bob even when confronting others goes against your grain. And the result was positive! You took the risk. You were thinking of Bob first, before yourself, even knowing Bob could have rejected you and become angry." Once again Julie affirmed me.

Before eating, Julie and I bowed our heads in prayer. We thanked our Heavenly Father for our evening meal, and for Bob and John, our brothers in Christ.

## JULIE MADE THE DIFFERENCE

From 1988-1992 Julie and I worked with Shelter Now International as volunteer relief workers in the Nasir Bagh refugee camp near Peshawar, Pakistan. I directed a milk distribution program for Afghan refugee children. Julie assisted in the work for the refugee women.

Because the Muslim Afghan men had such great respect for Julie, they respected me. This came about because Julie gladly chose to adapt to Afghan culture. She carefully observed the behavior of the Afghan women and adjusted herself to their ways. For example, this meant being fully wrapped by a large, sheet-like covering that reached below her knees over loose baggy pants and a blouse. Also, Julie had to have her head fully covered.

Men dominate the Afghan culture. The role of a woman is to be submissive and obedient, to take care of the man's needs, and to bear children. If the men did not think that I had full control of my wife, they would have no respect for me. Their respect for me depended on their respect for Julie. I had to be careful not to allow their Islamic culture to influence me regarding my wife.

Because the men came to fully trust Julie, at times they would want Julie to help their wives. Sometimes they would ask my manager of the milk distribution program, Abdul, to please ask me to ask my wife to visit their wife who was having an emotional or physical problem. Julie was always glad to help in this way.

After working in the refugee camp all day, it was our habit in the evening to drive again to the camp to visit our Afghan friends. It was not proper for Julie to look directly at the men or to acknowledge them when we got out of our vehicle. A little girl would meet Julie and lead her to the ladies' quarters. I would greet the men and accompany them to the men's tea house. We enjoyed these visits and looked forward to them.

One evening we visited as usual, but when I arrived at work the next morning the men approached me looking very serious. One of them said, "Mr. David, how is it that your wife speaks much better Pashtu than you do?" In the Afghan culture it is very shameful for a woman to be able to do something better than a man. The men had spoken to their wives after our visit the evening before. Their wives told them how very well Julie spoke Pashtu.

I looked seriously into their rugged faces and replied, "I can explain that. I am her teacher!"

Smiles broke out across their faces. I had redeemed myself.

Because of her adaptable behavior, Julie made the difference in opening the hearts of the Afghan men to me. Thank you, my love.

*Pakistan 1989*

# SAD AND LONELY

I wiped the sweat from my brow as I walked into our three-room house. I had just arrived home after a long hot day in the Nasir Bagh refugee camp near Peshawar, Pakistan. To my surprise, Julie was sitting in a wicker chair with a very sad look on her face. I plopped down in a chair near her. "What's wrong, Honey?" I asked. I knew something was disturbing my normally bubbly wife. I quietly waited for her to respond.

"David, I was left out again today when three of the mothers got together to have tea and to let their children play together. It seems it never occurs to them to invite me since we do not have children. They are good women and mean well, but it still hurts. At times I feel lonely."

I felt my wife's pain. After a long pause, Julie wiped the tears from her eyes. "Sweetheart, once a young mother jokingly said to me, 'You don't understand children because you don't have any.' I didn't think her words were funny, but I know that some people feel that way about us."

I wondered how some Christians at times could be so insensitive, actually cruel. I wanted to heal Julie's wounded heart. Silently I prayed, *Lord, you too feel her pain. Please pour your healing oil on her heart. You love her even more than I do.*

Finally, I responded, "Julie, it's sad that some people hold to such a false assumption. Honey, I have never met a person with greater understanding of children than you. You taught first graders for seven years. Those little ones adored you. You knew how to beautifully relate to them."

Julie smiled slightly and I continued.

"The other day this thought came to me. People say only a former alcoholic can really understand and relate to another alcoholic. But what about Jesus? He never sinned. Since He never sinned, does that mean He could not relate to sinners? It seems to me that since He never sinned, He could see more clearly than anyone else how horrible and destructive sin is. And what about David Wilkerson, the young country preacher who was raised in a pastor's home? In the eyes of others, he was Mr. Clean. God sent him to New York City to bring the Good News to drug addicts, alcoholics, gang members, and prostitutes. As a result, Teen Challenge was birthed, and thousands of troubled lives have been redeemed."

"David, that's worth thinking about," Julie reflected.

I sat there trying to figure out how to solve her problem. Then I remembered something I had read in a book. It pointed out that most husbands feel compelled to fix the problems their wives share with them. They do not realize it is more important to their wives to be genuinely heard and empathized with, than to solve their problems.

I thought, *David, you've got to remember that.* But, I admit, an idea that might help the situation did come to me.

"Julie, may I suggest that you consider inviting those three mothers over for tea and letting their children play in our yard? Maybe then it will occur to them to invite you the next time they get together."

"David, that's a good idea! I'll do just that."

I thought in my heart, *That's my Julie*. More than once I had seen her bounce back from disappointments and I knew why. She knew how to give her disappointments to the Lord.

*Pakistan 1990*

# WIDOWS CENTER IN PESHAWAR

The Pakistani chief administrator for the Nasir Bagh Afghan refugee camp located 20 minutes from Peshawar, Pakistan, sent word to me to come see him. At that time, I was the Shelter Now International (SNI) milk program director for Afghan refugee children. In that camp alone we provided milk five days a week to 10,000 children.

I immediately went to his office in the camp. Thin, middle-aged Mr. Ali and I had become friends. We greatly respected each other. As a Muslim student he had graduated from Gordon College in Peshawar, founded by Christian missionaries.

In Mr. Ali's sparse office I sat across from his desk and listened. "Mr. David, I need to discuss with you a serious problem we have in the camp. We now have many widows due to the war in Afghanistan. As you know, Afghans normally absorb widows into their extended families. However, due to the loss of so many men in the war, the number of widows has become so overwhelming that the families can no longer take care of all of them.

"As you know, we created an area of the camp that is reserved only for widows and their children. This has caused a major social problem. This is unacceptable because there are no male relatives to protect them. Mr. David, I know that your wife and her German colleague, Irmgard, have been informally visiting the widows and trying to help them in any way possible. May I make a suggestion?"

"Sure," I responded. "I can understand and appreciate the problem you face."

Mr. Ali continued, "I am aware that your wife and her colleague are culturally sensitive as they try to assist and encourage the widows. I would like your NGO* to consider building a special center for the widows. Your wife and her colleague could be the directors. I believe I can convince the United Nations to pay for such a project. What do you think?"

I smiled and answered, "Mr. Ali, we would like to do what we can to improve the situation for the widows. Please give me time to discuss this with my wife, her colleague, and the SNI leadership."

"Fine," he agreed.

We shook hands warmly as I left the office. I was excited to tell Julie and Irmgard about this request. As we discussed it, they thought it was a great idea and the SNI leadership agreed.

Julie and Irmgard carefully designed the center with high mud boundary walls that would ensure the

---

*NGO—A non-governmental organization: usually non-profit and independent from any government

widows' complete privacy. A number of garden plots would be laid out so each widow could have her own small garden. There would be a playground, especially designed with swings for the enjoyment of the children as well as the women. Classrooms would be constructed where they could use new sewing machines and be taught different skills. And, of course, there would be tea tables where the ladies could sit around and relax as they enjoyed each other's company.

The UN approved and funded the project. Soon the construction of the center began.

The SNI Afghan workers did a good job building the center. We all were very proud of their completed work.

Mr. Ali then summoned me to his office. "Mr. David, I need to tell you that the fanatics in the camp are very opposed to the center. They asked me not to allow the center to be opened. I told them the center will open since they did not give me any good reason why it should be closed."

"Mr. Ali," I responded, "Please invite their leaders to come to your office to meet with me. Tell them I will be glad to show them everything inside the new widows center and answer any questions they may have."

Mr. Ali sent word to them, but they refused to see me. Julie and Irmgard opened the center, knowing they would be taking a dangerous risk, since they would likely become targets for the fanatics. I knew the dangers they faced. The fanatics had murdered a talented Afghan doctor who lived in our neighborhood. Also, in our area they had shot and killed a good man because he had given an interview to a BBC reporter.

But Julie and I were convinced she and Irmgard were to reach out in the love of God to the widows who had terribly suffered the loss of loved ones. I was concerned for Julie and Irmgard and prayed daily for them. Since love compelled us, fear could not dominate us.

The widows bravely came to the center ignoring the threats of the fanatics. At times, while they were on their way to the center, they were cursed, and bigoted extremists threw stones at them.

Once inside the center they experienced peace, calmness, love and acceptance. These desperate women could pour out their sorrows to Julie and Irmgard who felt their pain. They could laugh together, relax, and be lighthearted. The center to them was like an oasis in a hot, dry desert. It gave them hope.

Julie would come home in the afternoons bubbling over with joy because of the special relationships she and Irmgard were establishing with the widows.

*Eid-al-Fitr,* a three-day Islamic holiday near the end of April, occurred about twelve weeks after the center opened. This is a celebration held at the end of Ramadan, the month of fasting. The first day of *Eid* is a family day for our Muslim friends. We looked forward to visiting them on the second and third days.

Unbeknown to us the fanatics had planned a riot for the first day of *Eid* since no foreigners would be in the camp and all the Pakistani officials would have gone to their villages. On that morning the fanatics stirred the people, formed a mob, and attacked the widows center. It was completely destroyed and everything inside was stolen. They also destroyed the Afghan girls school, sponsored by the Pakistani government, which was next to the widows center.

Then everything got out of control. The mob grew and broke into the SNI factory area and destroyed the forms used to construct the building components for shelters, clinics, and schools. They looted the vehicle workshop. The rioters broke into the warehouse where I had recently stored enough powdered milk to feed the refugee children for the next five months. Every bag of powdered milk was stolen. Total destruction took place. It would take 1.5 million dollars to replace the loss.

During the rioting many of the widows called out to the unrestrained rioters trying to shame them. No one listened.

Julie was totally heartbroken. She wept and wept. There were no funds to rebuild the center or any other work of SNI. Some Afghans held Julie responsible for the riot. They said the widows center had been built because of her and Irmgard's involvement. If there had not been a center, there wouldn't have been a riot.

But the widows knew who was responsible for the destruction. They knew who truly loved and cared for them. The fanatics could not destroy the love the widows experienced from devout Christians. Neither could they stop Julie's continuous prayers of intercession for her widowed friends she knew by name. She knew God loved them and He, not the insecure fanatics, would have the last word.

Julie and I had to leave Pakistan, but the love of God the widows experienced through Julie and Irmgard will always remain.

# HEARING THE LORD DIFFERENTLY

Two years after the riot at the Afghan refugee camp, Julie and I were again living in Peshawar, Pakistan, doing limited relief work. It was 9:00 in the evening. I said, "Julie, I sense the Lord wants to speak to me, but I have no idea what it could be about. I'm going to my study to meditate and pray. It has been a long day for you. Please go on to bed. I'll come later."

"Okay, that's fine." Julie gave me a kiss and left the room. I thoughtfully entered my study, closed the door, and sat down at my desk. I was perplexed, but I could sense the Presence of the Lord. For the next three hours I quietly sought the Lord. To my astonishment by the time I left my study, I knew the Lord had spoken to me that Julie and I were to leave Pakistan and move to the country then known as Czechoslovakia. I knew very little about Czechoslovakia except that young Afghan students were sent there by their Communist government to study.

The next morning when Julie and I had our devotions together I enthusiastically announced, "Sweetheart, the Lord spoke to me last night. We are to move to Czechoslovakia to minister particularly to Afghan students. This came as a complete surprise to me."

"That's a huge surprise alright!" Julie replied as she leaned forward in her chair. "Tell me about it."

I relaxed and told her how the Lord had spoken to me.

"David," Julie responded. "We can't go there. I don't even know how to spell the name of that country." We both laughed and she continued, "Well, it's marvelous the Lord has spoken to you. Now all we need are confirmations from the Holy Spirit. And I mean big confirmations."

As we continued to pray, the Holy Spirit did confirm we were to leave Pakistan and move to Czechoslovakia, which was later renamed the Czech Republic.

Although the Holy Spirit would speak to me differently than to Julie, she was not skeptical of my experiences. Neither did she feel threatened or intimidated because she did not hear His voice the same way I did. During our married life I have had dreams or visions or have heard the Holy Spirit speak to me as clearly as an audible voice, although it was not an audible voice. Julie has never had such experiences. However, we always carefully checked to be sure my experiences conformed to the Holy Bible, for no experience is above the Word.

What I believed God spoke to me had to be confirmed by Him to both of us. Otherwise we did not act on it. Julie was my safety net and kept me from making mistakes. I have the utmost confidence in her discernment and good judgment.

There have been times she has firmly questioned, "David, can you look me straight in the eye and say you know for certain it is the Holy Spirit telling you this? Is it a word from God, or is it just a great idea you have for God?" Sometimes I could not look her straight in the eye.

At times I knew the Lord spoke to me through Julie. Often she did not realize it, but I did. The Lord constantly speaks to Julie through the Scripture. Daily she reads the Bible. During the years we lived in Kandahar, Afghanistan, she prayerfully meditated through the whole Bible.

Although Julie and I hear from the Lord differently, we are thankful that we hear.

*Pakistan 1995*

# PLAN FOR THE FUTURE

Abdul, my faithful co-worker, and I were to travel south from Peshawar, Pakistan to Quetta, Pakistan, and then cross the border into Afghanistan. Then we would make our way to Kandahar. There we planned to meet with the Taliban and survey the needs of the people to see how we might be able to help with humanitarian aid. This trip would be risky and dangerous. I felt especially blessed to have my devout Afghan Muslim friend accompany me.

While I was gone Julie would stay in Islamabad, Pakistan with our close friend Donna Hardee. At that time Donna was a joyous single lady from the States who was serving our Lord there. She had a remarkable hospitality ministry to Pakistani ladies.

Before I left, I knew I needed to have a serious talk with Julie about her future in case something happened to me.

I said, "Sweetheart, you know I am going into a very dangerous situation. I am grateful to our Heavenly Father that although you are concerned about me when I'm in such circumstances, you don't worry about me. That takes a burden off my shoulders since then I don't have to worry about you worrying about me."

Julie smiled. "Well, David, we know the risks we take when we walk in obedience to our Lord. I always commit you into His hands and I know I can trust Him no matter what happens."

I constantly marveled at Julie's unshakeable faith. Her faith was based on the resurrection of the Lord Jesus and His reality in her life.

"What would you do if something happened to me?" I asked.

"David, I've never really thought about it."

"Sweetheart, I think it would be a good idea for us to talk about a plan."

Julie was quiet for a few moments before responding, "David, it's hard for me to think about life without you, but you're right. I need a plan."

"Honey, you are a marvelous missionary. It seems to me you should remain in missions. That's where your heart is."

"You're right. My heart is in missions. My calling to be a missionary would not change."

"Julie, I have a suggestion. If something happens to me, I suggest that you join Donna and minister with her. You and Donna are two peas in a pod. She's an incredible woman of God. You two would make a great team."

Julie smiled. "That's a great idea. Donna and I can talk heart to heart about anything. I love to hear her pray. Wow, David! Sometimes you can come up with outstanding ideas!"

"I try."

"David, your idea seems so right. But I hope I never have to implement that plan."

"I hope so too, but wisdom says we should be ready for any eventuality."

When Julie shared the idea with Donna, she wholeheartedly agreed.

As I fell asleep the night before leaving for Kandahar, peace filled my heart. I knew if God called me home unexpectedly, Julie had a plan and would courageously carry on.

*Ohio 1997*

## JULIE'S WISDOM BY MY FATHER'S GRAVE

On a hillside in the village of Augusta, Ohio, I solemnly stood by my father's grave. It had been three years since he had passed. It surprised me that I was still processing my grief. I was overseas when my father suddenly died of a heart attack. It saddened me that no one was with him at the time. Most of all, I felt the pain of not being able to say *goodbye*.

Knowing that my father never understood me made his passing extra hard. He was a self-absorbed man who did not know how to raise a son. I often longed to have a great relationship with my father, but it never happened. I had served the Lord many years overseas before my father ever asked me any questions about my experiences. Now, as I stood by his grave, tears filled my eyes. I felt deep sorrow because I knew what a marvelous father-son relationship we could have had.

I had asked Julie to please wait and let me be alone for a while at my father's grave before she joined me. When she did join me, she said, "I know, David, that your father failed you in major ways. But let's think about the good things you learned from him, things that have helped you in life. For example, your father taught you to never tell a lie. Because your father never took an alcoholic drink, neither have you. You never smoked a cigarette since your father never smoked. You told me you never heard your father swear or tell an off-color story, therefore neither did you. Your father taught you never to cheat another person, so you haven't. He faithfully gave his tithe to the church from every paycheck. So from the first dollar you ever earned, you have always done the same. He taught you a commendable work ethic. From the time you were born, he saw to it that you faithfully attended church.

"David, I think it will be helpful if you remember the positive things you inherited from your father."

I looked into Julie's soft tender eyes as she gently squeezed my hand. Tears again filled my eyes as I silently thought about what she said. I had been so deeply hurt by my father's major negative faults that I had not seen his positive influence as I should have.

After a long quiet silence on that beautiful hillside graced with lovely trees, Julie whispered, "David, let's kneel and pray." So we knelt in the green grass by my father's grave.

I was too overwhelmed emotionally to pray.

Julie began praying. I have never heard a more beautiful prayer. She thanked our Savior for all the good things I had learned from my father. As she prayed, my Heavenly Father wonderfully healed me. When we rose from our knees, I knew my grieving was over.

As we walked hand in hand to our car, I knew I would see my father again. My wise brother-in-law, Ray Miller, had ministered to my father and helped my father realize he needed to repent of some very grievous issues. Before his death, my father truly repented and asked for forgiveness.

Before getting into the car, Julie and I stood and looked again down the hill at my father's grave. A bird chirped in a nearby tree. It was as if that happy bird knew the peace I was experiencing.

Julie smiled and said, "You know, David, when you get to heaven your father will finally understand you, and you will have that relationship with him that you always wanted."

Tears of joy flowed as I realized what my precious wife said was true.

## THE NEW NEIGHBORS

In October, 1997, Julie and I arrived in Kandahar, Afghanistan, the headquarter city of the Taliban in southern Afghanistan. By that time the fanatical Taliban

had taken Kabul, the capital of Afghanistan. We were
invited by an Afghan NGO* to work with them. They
made and provided prostheses so those who lost a leg
from stepping on a mine could walk again. I told the
kind, young Afghan NGO director that we were devout
Christians sponsored by the church and friends. I gave
him a copy of our book *Afghanistan, My Tears* to read
so he and his assistant would know whom they were
inviting. I said to the two men, "You need to be sure you
want us because the Taliban could become very unhappy
with you." They assured me there would be no problem
since we both wanted to serve God.

Three weeks after our arrival in Kandahar there was
a problem. Tremendous pressure was asserted on the
NGO leader. To protect their project, I resigned. But
God did a miracle. The Taliban gave me permission to
stay and become the director of a precast roofing beam
factory sponsored by Shelter Now International (SNI).
For the next two years Julie and I lived in Kandahar
under the rule of the Taliban.

For the first five months we lived in one room,
located in the servants' quarters on the compound of
the United Nations High Commission for Refugees
(UNHCR). Eventually we rented a two-story house
across the street. The front of the house became my
official office. The back part of the house was our
private living quarters. Inside the house a solid brick
wall was constructed to divide our living quarters from
the office because Julie had to be secluded.

Julie was not permitted to visit Afghan women, nor
were they allowed to come to her. Fortunately, our

---

*NGO—*A non-governmental organization: usually non-profit and
independent from any government*

flat-roofed house was surrounded by a 12-foot-high mud boundary wall. This enabled Julie to enjoy the large backyard. She had her own office in the private part of the house where she assisted me with my administrative work.

Along both sides of the house was a walkway. To separate the front office from our house in the back, we installed gates to comply with Taliban rules made to "protect Julie's privacy." No one was permitted beyond the gates.

I requested the Taliban's permission for Abdul, my office manager and personal assistant, as well as our cook, Farid; our house helper, Munir; and our *chowkidar* (day guard), Sher Gul, to be allowed to go into the back area of our compound and into our house when needed. I told the Taliban this permission was necessary in order for me to carry out my work. Reluctantly they granted permission.

Our new neighbors, a father with four small children, lived on the other side of the west boundary wall. They lived in the rubble of a house. Only one small, damaged room remained.

Under Taliban rule, all second-floor house windows had to be painted to prevent anyone from looking into a neighbor's yard. Julie could hear the children playing on the other side of our wall. She scratched off just enough paint from the window to see out, yet not enough to be noticeable. She could then look into the yard and see the children.

By looking into the yard below, Julie soon realized the children were sleeping on the ground with nothing but the worn-out clothes on their backs. She said to me, "We have to do something about this." I agreed.

I sent Abdul next door to learn more about our new neighbors. He returned to tell us a sad story.

The mother had died a month after giving birth to her fourth child, a son named Daoud. Daoud was now two years old. The oldest child was a seven-year-old girl named Spogmay. Her sister, Mina, was five and another brother, Zaman, was four. Their father, Ali Madad, who had lost one eye, was ill with a terrible cough, and had no work.

"Mr. David," Abdul lamented, "this family is desperately poor. They are surviving only on stale naan* that other Afghans give them."

"Abdul, this is horrible," Julie said as tears formed in her eyes.

I responded, "Abdul, please make a list of this family's basic needs."

Abdul's list included teacups and a tea kettle to boil water; some cooking pans and utensils; locally worn plastic shoes for each family member and material for new clothes; cotton-filled sleeping mats and cots to get them off the ground (snakes and scorpions were common); and mosquito nets to sleep under to protect them from malaria-carrying mosquitoes in the area.

I sent Abdul to the bazaar to buy all these items.

On his return he took the supplies to the family. They were overjoyed. The children jumped up and down and squealed. Ali Madad said he couldn't believe strangers could be so kind. Julie and I were thrilled to know that the little family would no longer be sleeping on the ground and had what they needed. Following

---

*A whole-wheat flatbread usually baked in a tandoor, a round clay oven

our instructions our cook, Farid, each day quietly provided nourishing food.

## Julie's Joy

Most of my days in Kandahar were spent with Abdul at my side. There were people to meet who came to the factory. There was work at the factory that needed supervision, UN and NGO meetings to attend, and discussions with Taliban officials. I enjoyed the interactions.

Life for Julie had a different focus. She was confined to our house and the backyard. Once a week on our day off I took her for a ride in our double-cab pickup truck. Following the Taliban's instructions, she had to sit in the back seat and, of course, she wore her long black, sheetlike covering and dark sunglasses. But just being out of the compound gave her a change in scenery and a chance to see folks on the roads and in the surrounding countryside.

At home Julie interacted with our house helper, Munir, who had served us for 15 years. Together they worked improving the house. They made plans and Munir would go to the bazaar to find the items needed to implement their ideas. He went to the carpenter shop, explained their design for curtain fixtures, and had the wooden support rods made. In the bazaar Munir found material samples to bring back so Julie could choose just the right patterns. Then he bicycled off to the tailor to explain how the material should be sewn. None of the procedures moved quickly, but projects were eventually finished.

Julie worked with our cook, Farid, planning meals which were made from scratch with seasonal fruits, vegetables and meat he purchased in the bazaar. We fed not only ourselves, but also our staff who lived in the office area at the front of the compound and the family next door.

In the evenings Julie and I always had things to talk about and regularly took time for prayer and worship.

I was constantly amazed at Julie's joyfulness. I knew it was the result of her relationship with the Lord, coupled with the strong conviction that it was His will for us to be in Kandahar.

Julie is a people person. She loves to be with others, to share, and to serve. Yet by God's grace she is content when that isn't possible. However, in Kandahar God made it possible for her to have a delightful relationship with the children from over the wall. Spogmay, who was seven years old when we met her, was "little mama." She looked after the children, especially the smallest one, Daoud. She walked regally straight and even at her young age had a strong bearing. She was stoic, had calm, dark brown eyes, was not quick to smile, and was quite intelligent.

Two-year-old Daoud, seemed just the opposite. He followed his siblings and believed he could do whatever they did. He flopped around in plastic boots and often suffered some kind of wound from falling or running into something. He didn't talk much, but it was apparent he saw everything.

In the middle were sweet five-year-old Mina and adventurous four-year-old Zaman. Mina appeared to be gentle, compliant, and quietly happy. She and her big sister were close, good friends. Zaman liked to be outside his compound squatting next to his father, observing what was happening on the dirt-packed street.

The children's day usually started early, not long after sunrise. Unless it was raining, we often heard them playing in their compound. From our bedroom Julie peeked through the peephole to see them performing their childhood antics. Then, usually laughing, she would relate to me what they were doing. One morning Zaman pretended to be a mullah, standing with head upward, hands cupped around his mouth making the call to prayer.

On another morning they all played wedding. They marched about the compound making music on their yellow plastic water-jug drums. They sang and danced like they would at a traditional wedding. They didn't know singing and dancing were now forbidden by the Taliban. Wow! What fun they had!

Farid, Abdul, Munir and Sher Gul each adopted the family and quietly looked after them. Abdul often stopped to talk with Ali Madad as he sat leaning against the wall outside his compound.

Ali Madad was thin and often coughing. We suspected he had tuberculosis.

"Abdul, we need to take Ali Madad to a clinic. I am concerned about his coughing," I expressed to Abdul one morning.

Our suspicions were confirmed. Ali Madad was diagnosed with TB.

"Abdul, we will buy the expensive medicines needed for him to get well," I said.

That was the beginning of a yearlong regimen of multiple-drug therapy and regular check-ups at the clinic.

Abdul made sure the medicine was available and Ali Madad faithfully took it. At the end of a year there was great rejoicing when he was declared free of TB.

To prepare for the Muslim holiday of Eid-al-Fitr at the end of the month of fasting called Ramadan, everyone tries to have new clothes to wear. Abdul went to the bazaar to buy cloth for new outfits for the children. The tailor made shalwar-kameezes for Spogmay and Mina using a light green fabric with pink flowers. Zaman proudly strutted around in his new solid-brown shalwar-kameez. Daoud followed Zaman around, wearing an identical suit and green plastic boots. Because the weather was cool, we gave the girls green woolen shawls. From a popular used-clothing bazaar, Abdul purchased a blue sweater and stocking hat for Zaman and a purple hooded jacket for Daoud. On the day of the holiday the children slipped into our compound to joyfully show Julie their new clothes.

She could hardly keep back tears of joy. All the men on staff smiled big.

A highlight of Julie's days was the children's visits.

Just inside our walled compound gate we had a safe water well with a faucet. The children in the neighborhood often banged on the large gate wanting to come in to fill their plastic water containers. Sher Gul, our grey-bearded watchman, was a patient man who loved children. He would open the small door in the gate and let them in.

Our four neighbor children came every day with the other neighborhood children. This is how it came about that they could enter our compound. Julie arranged with Sher Gul to let them in three days a week at the end of the day after the other children had gone. He would lock the gate and summon Julie. She would slip around to the front of our house properly covered as an Afghan lady. After the children filled their water containers, they would sit up straight on a white bench on our concrete porch with their feet dangling. Julie sat across from them. They knew Julie would give them Tang orange drink and another treat, usually a homemade cookie. As Julie chatted with the children in Pashtu, they basked in this special attention, knowing she loved them.

"David, these are beautiful-looking kids, but they sure need to be scrubbed up. I can't initiate that, but I really would like to," Julie moaned.

"Be patient," I replied. "Let's see what happens."

One hot day after their visit with Julie, as they headed toward the gate and were about to walk past the faucet, Zaman turned it on and stuck his head under the cool flowing water.

"Don't let them go," Julie called to Sher Gul. She raced back to our part of the house and immediately returned with a bottle of shampoo and a comb. Zaman giggled as he rubbed the bubbly shampoo into his matted hair. Then they all wanted to join the fun. Soon Julie was combing their clean hair.

When she finished, she shouted to Sher Gul, "Don't let them go yet." Again, she ran around to the back of our house and returned with a small mirror. Julie kept

telling the children how great they looked with such
lovely hair. They stood a little taller, just
a little proud, admiring themselves in the mirror.

"You can come anytime to wash your hair," Julie
encouraged them. They nodded approvingly and
walked out carrying their new comb and mirror.
After that Julie made sure Sher Gul had a supply
of shampoo, a comb, and a mirror ready for use.

## We Know

The day came when I received an urgent request
from our international director, Georg Taubmann. The
SNI country director for Afghanistan had to suddenly
leave the country due to a serious heart condition.
*Could I please move to Kabul as soon as possible to replace him?*
It was a tough decision, but I knew I owed this to SNI.
So Julie and I prepared to move.

The day before we departed, I sadly walked across
the dusty street to the UNHCR compound. It was
exactly two years after our arrival in Kandahar. I
went to say goodbye to the Afghan men who worked
there. As I was leaving Mr. Jaweed, the gentleman who
had kindly given us a room on the UNHCR compound
when we first arrived in Kandahar, walked along beside
me. He was also in charge of the men who worked on
the grounds—the gardeners, watchmen, etc.

"Mr. David, may I have a word with you before
you leave?"

"Of course, Mr. Jaweed."

"Mr. David, I want you to know we know what you and your wife have done all this time for the children who live next to you. We know, Mr. David, we know. We want to say thank you."

Tears welled up in my eyes. I was deeply moved.

"You're welcome, Mr. Jaweed. It was our privilege to do so."

Mr. Jaweed warmly shook my hand with both of his.

"May God bless you, Mr. Jaweed."

"And you," he replied.

I walked across the street and into our house. "Julie," I called. "I have something to tell you. I've just spoken with Mr. Jaweed. He and his men thanked us for taking care of the children. He said they have known all along what we have been doing."

"Wow!" Julie said. "And we tried so hard to keep it concealed from the Taliban."

"Yes we did and so did they. Not one of those men informed the Taliban during the two years we've been here."

Julie smiled and said, "Sweetheart, may God bless those men!"

I smiled too, for I believed He would.

## Heartbroken

The night before we left Kandahar Julie sobbed and wailed. I thought her heart would break. I had never seen my beautiful wife react in such a way. My own eyes were shedding tears because of the heartache of having to leave the four children living next to us. They had stolen our hearts. We could not imagine leaving them in such a situation. We were glad their one-eyed father had completely recovered from TB, but he was still unemployed. Now who would take care of these precious children?

In the morning their father, Ali Madad, slipped them unnoticed through our gate to say goodbye. The children said they would come to see us in Kabul. They had no idea about distance; they thought Kabul was nearby. As we hugged them, Julie and I tried to put on our best smiles and attempted not to appear sad, even though inside our hearts were breaking. We stooped down to their eye level and told them we would ask God to protect and keep them.

Ali Madad tried to thank us the best way he could for all we had done for him and his family. He, too, was having a hard time controlling his emotions. Then he slipped his family out the gate carrying containers of water so it would look like a routine visit.

## Big Surprise Ten Years Later!

Late one Saturday afternoon our Afghan workers had gone home after another blistering hot day of successfully repairing another water well in a village about an hour from Jalalabad. The men were tired but happy. It was a good start to a new work week.

Abdul stayed behind to visit with me. We went to my house and sat under a large shade tree. Fortunately,

we had electricity at that time and the big portable fan
worked. Cool water quenched our thirst.

After taking a long drink of water, Abdul asked,
"Mr. David, could Julie sit with us today? I have
something very important to tell both of you."

"Certainly," I said. I went into the house and asked
Julie to join us.

After Abdul politely greeted Julie and she was
seated, he began: "Yesterday, while in the bazaar, I met
one of our SNI workers from our factory in Kandahar.
I met him once a long time ago, but I did not recognize
him at first.

"However, he knew who I was. His name is Jamil.
He was hired as a new worker at our factory about a
month after we left. He lives in Kandahar but recently
came to visit his uncle who is ill. I invited him to have
tea with me. He asked about you."

"Abdul, why would he ask about me? I never met
the man," I wondered.

"That puzzled me also, so I politely asked him why
he was asking about Mr. David. He replied, 'Do you
know a man named Ali Madad who has four children
and lived next to Mr. David in Kandahar?'

"Yes, I knew him well," I responded, "but I never
knew what happened to him and his family after we
left Kandahar. Do you know him?

"Then Jamil explained, 'I met him several months
after Mr. David moved from Kandahar. One day
he appeared at the factory and asked us if we knew
how Mr. David was doing. We asked him why he was
inquiring about him. He said Mr. David had provided

the medicine which enabled him to recover from
TB. We told him that was good. Then he continued
and said that Mrs. David was the mother of his four
children for two years when they had no mother.'

"Jamil said Ali was grateful to God for you both and
he hoped you were well."

Julie and I leaned forward. It had been ten years
since we left Kandahar. We never knew what happened
to Ali Madad and his children.

"Abdul, did Jamil say anything else about Ali Madad
and the children?"

"Yes," Abdul responded. "Jamil said about every five
or six months, Ali Madad appeared at the factory asking
about Mr. and Mrs. David. He always wanted to know if
they were okay. Jamil would always tell him they had not
heard from Mr. David. Jamil told me only three weeks ago
Ali Madad once again appeared inquiring about you."

Julie and I were completely dumbfounded. It was
hard to believe that Ali Madad kept coming to ask about
us. Over the years we had kept in touch with the main
SNI office in Kabul. It was hard to believe that Ali
Madad's visits to the factory were never communicated
to the Kabul office by the Kandahar workers.

"Abdul, did Jamil tell you about Ali Madad and
his family?"

"Mr. David, I knew you and Julie would want to
know. I asked him to tell me anything he knew. Ali
Madad told him that after you left, Mr. Malik, your
landlord, not only immediately cut the one electric line
you had provided for his family, he also threatened to
have the Taliban take his children if he did not move

someplace else within three days. Fortunately, Ali
Madad found a room in another ruined house."

When Abdul told me that, my face flushed with
anger. I wanted to ask God to destroy all of Mr.
Malik's properties.

Abdul continued, "Jamil said Ali Madad began
repairing bicycles on the street in front of his place.
He also found a wife and a mother for his children.
Eventually he opened his own bicycle repair shop. His
two sons assist him and are doing well."

Julie asked, "How are his daughters, Spogmay
and Mina?"

"They are now engaged to be married next year to
two brothers."

Julie slumped back in her chair. Tears began
to rapidly spill from her eyes. My own eyes were
flooded with tears. It was as if a dam had broken
within us. Tears also began slowly streaming down
Abdul's cheeks.

Abdul finally spoke, "Jamil will return to Kandahar
in another week. I have his cell phone number. I told
him you would want to send a message through him to
Ali Madad. He said he would be happy to give it."

In the weeks ahead, Abdul and I did everything
possible to make arrangements to see Ali Madad and
his children. Nothing worked. It was too dangerous
for them to have us visit them in Kandahar, and it was
too dangerous and complicated for them to visit us in
Jalalabad. We would pray and wait. God had faithfully
protected the family we loved even when at times we
wondered if our prayers were being effective.

*Afghanistan 1998*

# THE ROBBERY IN KANDAHAR

Julie and I rushed to the Red Cross office in Kabul. That morning we received word that our house in Kandahar was robbed the night before. We arrived just in time to catch a ride to the Bagram air base north of Kabul. From there we flew south on a small Red Cross plane to Kandahar.

When we arrived at our house we were relieved to know that none of our men were hurt. Afghans have the habit of not wanting to tell you any bad news that would make you sad or upset. Therefore, we did not know if any of our staff had been injured or even killed during the robbery. With the men who worked with us, we stood outside our house surrounded by high boundary walls. Our cook Farid's eyes were full of sadness. Sher Gul our *chowkidar* (day guard), looked down at his sandals. Munir, our broad-faced helper wiped sweat from his brow.

Abdul, my office manager, took a deep breath and said, "Mr. David, we are so very sorry about the robbery. Apparently in the middle of the night the thieves came over the back wall and managed to get the back door of the house open. They stole many things. We never heard them. Munir normally gets up in the night but, for some strange reason, never woke up once last night. In fact, for some unusual reason all of us slept soundly."

I smiled slightly. I knew, for their safety, Who had made them sleep soundly.

Abdul continued, "We know who the thieves are."

Looking baffled, I asked, "Who are they?"

Abdul pointed to the wall on the east side of our house. "They are the gang of thieves who moved three days ago into the empty house on the other side of our boundary wall. They are protected by the Taliban. Mr. David, we are going to have to move."

"Why?"

"Because in our culture when you are outnumbered by those who oppose you, you are the ones who have to move. Believe me, Mr. David, they outnumber us."

Julie, wrapped in what looked like a big black sheet which covered her from head to toe and who is normally quiet in the presence of men, suddenly spoke in a determined voice, "We are not moving. They are!"

She quickly turned, faced the east boundary wall that separated us from the thieves' house, raised her hands straight out before her toward their house, and said very loudly, "In the name of the Lord Jesus, you are out of here!" Then she marched into our house leaving us men standing there, stunned.

I decided to follow Julie into the house and went to my private office. The outside wall was about four feet from the boundary wall of the thieves' house. I sat there pondering what to do. Suddenly Julie appeared in the office doorway. She walked over and opened all the windows as wide as she could. Next she went to our CD player, inserted a Christian worship CD, and turned up the music as loudly as possible. Then I noticed she had a tambourine in her hand. I never knew she even owned one. I wondered where it came from. Next she marched around the office singing praises to God at the top of her voice while loudly beating the black tambourine.

I sat in total amazement thinking, *Oh, no, what is this wife of mine doing? She knows the Taliban harshly punish anyone who plays music.* I expected the Taliban to show up at any time to arrest us. Once in the past they had suddenly appeared at our front door when they realized the owner of the house had brought his wife to visit us. They harshly ordered them to leave immediately. The visiting couple fled like mice being chased by a cat.

I watched Julie march around the room again. I finally recovered from my shock enough to ask, "Julie, what in the world are you doing!?"

"I am praising God. I want those thieves to hear me and know I am not afraid. They are the ones who will move. Not us."

Three mornings later we awakened early to discover that the thieves were gone!

From that time on our faithful Afghan workers wanted Julie, instead of me, to pray for them! This did nothing for my ego, but then again, she was the bold one.

*1998*

# DON'T JUST STAND THERE!

It was another boiling hot day in Kandahar, Afghanistan. At the airport Julie sat on the tarmac with the Afghan women near the obviously antiquated airplane. The Taliban were in charge. The women were sweltering under their burqas* that completely covered them from head to toe. The only women who were not required to have their faces completely covered were the much older women who were considered beyond their prime. Julie was one of those. With only her face visible, Julie was totally wrapped in what looked like a big black sheet.

I stood with the group of men a good distance away from the women as we waited to board the aircraft. I kept wiping the sweat from my brow. I was dressed in Afghan clothes like I normally wore called *shalwar kameeze*, a long sleeved-shirt which reaches below the knees over big baggy pants. I also wore a white skull cap as part of the national dress.

We waited for more than an hour before the boarding began. The women took their seats in the back section of the plane and the men in the front. I had just gotten myself comfortably seated when I heard Julie loudly yelling, "David! David! David!"

I stood up and turned to try to locate her. When I saw Julie, she was standing facing a square-shouldered, muscular Pashtun man blocking him from sitting between her and a Pashtun woman. As far as I knew he had no business trying to sit in the women's area.

Julie yelled again, "David, don't just stand there, do something!"

I wanted to shout out for everyone to hear, "Look, folks, I don't know that woman!"

Against my better judgment I stepped out into the narrow aisle and started back towards Julie. I thought, *"What a way to die, but I am committed to her."*

*A loose tentlike covering from head to toe with mesh over the eyes. Often blue.

Right before I reached my place of death, Julie permitted this giant of a man to take the middle seat.

Julie smiled at the shocked look on my face. "Sweetheart, it's okay. The lady in the burqa just now whispered to me that he's her husband."

I returned to my seat thinking, *When I married this girl, I don't remember signing up for this. But on the other hand, life is not boring being married to the girl of my dreams.*

*1998*

# DISCOURAGEMENT

I sat soberly in my favorite chair as Julie poured two cups of hot tea and sat down across from me. It was the end of a long day. I had returned from the precast-concrete roofing beam factory which I directed for Shelter Now International on the edge of Kandahar, Afghanistan. I sat silently. Julie and I now had lived one and a half years under the Taliban. Kandahar was their headquarters city. Mullah Omar, the leader of the Taliban, lived five blocks from us. The year was 1998.

Julie saw the discouragement written on my face, but it wasn't the kind of discouragement most people would suspect. It was not because of where we lived. We never considered Kandahar a hard place even though most people would think it was. That was because Julie and I knew the joy of obeying our Lord. We knew this was where God wanted us to be.

Julie tenderly asked, "David, why do you look so sad and discouraged?"

I remained quiet for several moments. Finally I answered, "Today I have been thinking. For many years we've lived among our Muslim Afghan friends. We love them deeply and are glad to serve them. Many of them truly love and admire us. But they will not respond to the Good News that will assure them a place in heaven, as well as enable them to experience the love and peace of Christ as they walk on this earth. This breaks my heart. At times it seems to me all our efforts to bless our friends have been futile. But you know, Honey, if I could choose to do it all over again, I would choose to do the same as we have done."

Julie smiled. "I know you would, and so would I. That's one reason why I dearly love you."

"Honey, at times my heart is full of pain for our Muslim friends. Not for myself, but because I know what our dear friends are missing in life and will miss in the life to come. I would gladly give my life for them." Tears surfaced in my eyes.

"I know you would. As you have so often said, we don't truly love our Muslim friends if we don't care about their eternal destination."

I wept.

After I dried my tears, Julie softly said, "The love of Christ compels us and we will continue on."

*2003*

# RUSSIA

In April, 2000, Julie and I moved from Afghanistan, where we lived under the Taliban, to Cyprus, near Larnaca. We did not want to leave Afghanistan, the land of our calling, but we moved in obedience to our Lord. To our amazement God provided for us a small, inexpensive rental house on the Mediterranean Sea. From 2000 to 2003, we traveled to former Communist countries in Central and Eastern Europe and the former Soviet Union where I was a guest lecturer, usually for two or three weeks in each of the newly created Bible colleges. Of course flexible Julie was the oil in my motor that caused everything to run smoothly.

Then the unexpected happened. God made it clear that we were to move to Yekaterinburg, Russia, on the edge of Siberia, to minister to the former Soviet soldiers who had fought in Afghanistan. Adjustable Julie and I made preparations to do so.

On the morning of May 22, 2003, the day before my 61st birthday, Julie and I sat thoughtfully by the peaceful Mediterranean Sea. The sun glistened on the water. "So, Julie," I said, "are we really ready to give up our home in Cyprus and journey to Russia when all we can get are three-month visas? That means we will have to leave Russia every three months for an extended period before we can again obtain another three-month visa. That would make it extremely difficult to establish a ministry for the veterans."

With a twinkle in her eyes Julie smiled and replied, "Why, David, should we live differently now than we always have? We have always taken the risks and God has always been faithful."

I wanted to jump up, hug my wife, and shout to the world, "That's my Julie!"

We took the necessary steps of faith and flew to Yekaterinburg. When our three-month visas were soon to expire, a godly Russian lady, a member of the Russian church that sponsored our visas, took our passports to the police department that handled visas. She boldly approached the tough no-nonsense, dark-haired police official in charge, "Sir, I believe God sent these people here." She handed him a Russian copy of our book *Afghanistan, My Tears*. "Sir, please extend their visas."

He simply replied, "I believe God did." And he extended our visas. This he did two more times. Later we were granted one-year visas time and again.

We experienced five fruitful years ministering to the veterans of the Soviet/Afghan War. My heart still rejoices at Julie's words, "Why, David, should we live differently now than we always have?"

## BUT GOD, I REALLY LIKE HIM!

In 2012 Julie and I moved to Waxahachie, Texas. We were invited to mentor the students at Southwestern Assemblies of God University who felt called to serve our Savior in the Islamic world. This we did for three years.

One time I was again invited to be the chapel speaker to the student body at SAGU. As Julie and I sat in our little apartment she said, "David, don't get up there and just challenge the students. They are constantly being challenged. Get up there and make clear to them how they can live out the Christian life day by day. Make sure you have good illustrations that demonstrate practical applications." Again, I was experiencing direct counsel from my wife.

"Okay, Julie, since you seem to know how this is to be done, I am going to ask Dr. Paul Brooks to have you speak in my place."

Suddenly Julie was very quiet. After a long pause, in a soft voice she responded, "Okay, I will."

At that moment she had experienced a clear impression from the Holy Spirit that she should indeed be the speaker. She would obey the Lord even though she does not consider herself to be a gifted speaker and prefers not to be in front of others.

Dean Brooks graciously gave Julie permission to take my place. When the day came for her to speak, I had the joy of introducing her.

Julie walked to the microphone, stood silently looking over the student body, then raising her right hand, she looked up towards heaven and loudly said, "But God, I really like him. He is such a wonderful young man!"

Instantly it seemed every student moved to the edge of her or his seat. One girl immediately texted a friend who was skipping chapel, "Get over here! A romance story is being told!"

Under the anointing of the Holy Spirit, Julie in practical ways demonstrated how a person can daily experience living out the Christian life. Afterwards faculty members and students kept commenting to me about what an insightful and powerful message Julie had given.

Later I teasingly said to Julie, "Now when I go on campus students say to me, 'Julie we know, but who are you?'"

In a class I taught, Julie gave a lecture from history about the lives of wives of well-known missionaries. During her lecture Julie stated, "You know, I am not the wife of a missionary." Then, pausing for a moment, she said, "I'm a missionary wife. There's a difference."

Later when I gave an exam including questions from Julie's lecture to my surprise not one student missed one question taken from her lecture. I couldn't believe it. That was not the norm regarding my lectures. I said to Julie, "Life is so unfair!" She just smiled broadly.

While at SAGU I had the privilege of being the chaplain for the college basketball team. At the games Julie would sit directly behind the players and enthusiastically cheer them on.

It was a pleasure to have those wonderful players come over to our apartment for a meal. They loved Julie. She was always so upbeat with them. They loved her sense of humor. These young men liked to talk about girls, of course, and to seek out Julie's advice. Once a towering player, whose muscles were like iron, seriously spoke with Julie about marriage. He was concerned to meet and marry the right godly girl like Julie. During the end of their conversation Julie suggested, with a gleam in her eyes, "Be observant! Observe! Observe! Observe!" They laughed together.

Later, on campus when he would see Julie, he would say, "I'm observing! Observing! Observing!"

It was humorous to me when those tall young men would thank Julie for a delicious dinner as they bent way down to hug my five-foot one-inch wife.

How could I help but love Julie who made every player feel uniquely important?

I'm glad Julie told God years ago, "But God, I really like him."

## MACEDONIA

Sunday evening, August 30, 2015, Julie and I received an email from Brian and Colleen Thomas who were serving as missionaries on the border of Macedonia and Greece. It stated, "David and Julie, since you are now retired missionaries living in Springfield please come and join us. We need your help. Thousands of refugees are crossing into Macedonia each day. We are overwhelmed trying to assist them. Things are chaotic. Please pray about joining us. Most of the refugees are from Syria and perhaps 40% are Afghans."

After reading the email, I printed it and walked into the living room to share it with Julie.

"Well, Julie, I know we said we are not going any place this year because I need to finish writing the book *Abdul and Mr. Friday*. But we need to pray about this since it's a special request from our good friends Brian and Colleen."

"But David, you know we are committed to staying home for many reasons. God will have to make it crystal clear if He wants us to join them."

"I agree. I have an idea. Let's give God until midnight tomorrow night--Monday night. By then He will have to do something extraordinary, like us receiving a phone call completely out of the blue."

"Sounds great," Julie responded. We bowed our heads in prayer, placing this fleece before God.

Monday came and went. Nothing happened. Julie felt relieved and I thought *well, that's that . . .* and went about working on the book.

Then *out of the blue* on Wednesday afternoon my missionary friend, John Michno, called me from Greece. I had not been in touch with John for several years. The last I knew, he and his wife were in Russia. I had no idea they were in Greece.

John said, "You and Julie are needed out here to assist because many of the refugees are Afghans."

I responded, "John, you're two days too late."

"But, David!" John protested, "The Holy Spirit spoke to me last Friday to call you on Monday. But I failed to do so because I became too busy on Monday."

"John, are you telling me the truth?"

"Honest, David, I'm telling you the absolute truth. You can ask my wife." John had no idea that Brian and Colleen had already contacted us.

Julie was on her way to the beauty shop and had stepped into the hallway when she heard me answer the phone and say, "John, did you say you're calling from Greece?"

Upon hearing those words, she broke into tears and exclaimed, "My life has just changed. We are going to Macedonia."

Julie kept her appointment with her hairdresser. She walked into the shop crying.

"What's wrong, Julie? What's wrong?" her friend anxiously asked.

"My life has just changed. We're going to Macedonia to assist the refugees."

"Julie, can I go with you? I can do the refugee women's hair."

Julie smiled and said, "Robin, what a beautiful, compassionate heart you have."

Julie came home and we began our preparations for Macedonia.

Brian and Colleen met us at the airport. Soon another wonderful colleague named Daryl Pack came from the States to join us. Daryl is absolutely fluent in Arabic and loves Muslims. As a team each morning we distributed food packets to the refugees as they came through the gate into the United Nations receiving camp. Often thousands arrived daily.

In the afternoons we helped orientate the refugees to the camp. The Macedonian police were grateful for us since we helped to keep the refugees calm and assisted in giving directions. Daily I carried small children. Julie knew how to comfort the mothers. Their plight was heartbreaking, especially for the Syrians who did not want to leave their country. Nearly all the refugees were Muslims.

They were gracious when we politely asked if they would like us to pray with them. They would gladly say, "Please do," and would sincerely thank us. There were times when they asked us to share with them our Christian faith.

God gave Julie favor with the police, the refugee women, and the single young men. Since Julie was 72, it seemed the women and the single young men saw her as a mother or grandmother figure. She lifted their spirits because she was so positive and cheerful, plus she could be so humorous. Yet at the same time they knew Julie keenly felt their pain. It was amusing to them, and to me, to see energetic Julie quickly moving from place to place as she stopped to encourage a distressed mother, find clothes for the children, give assurances about the bus and train schedules, help to keep people organized, or serve as a go-between for the refugees and the police.

Once a Pashtun husband wanted to leave the camp to visit his wife who the day before had been taken to a hospital in town to give birth to a baby. He could speak only Pashtu. Julie translated for him. She convinced the police, because they trusted her, to give him permission to go to the hospital and then helped to arrange transportation for him.

After nearly two months of serving in the camp, we needed to return to the States. It was difficult to leave these suffering people. Our last day in the camp a group of Afghan single young men approached Julie with a special request. They said, "Miss Julie, could you please ask the police if we could do our national dance? We miss our homeland so very much."

Julie responded, "Sure, I'll try."

Although the police had doubts about this, winsome Julie convinced them, and they granted permission. I believe that happened because of their respect for my wife.

An area was cleared. Some policemen stood by curiously observing. The Afghan young men made a big circle. They began their national dance with special stepping and clapping. I stood by Julie as we both cried. Our hearts too traveled back to Afghanistan.

On the flight home I held Julie's hand while she slept. I thought, *what a wife I have! Always ready to drop everything and ready to go wherever God leads us.*

I looked over at Julie. She had a peaceful smile on her face. I wondered if I had married an angel.

*2018*

# FUNERAL PLANNING

It was a lovely fall evening in Springfield, Missouri. Julie and I especially enjoy autumn in the Ozarks. We like the crisp cool air and watching the leaves of the trees turn into radiant colors.

We were peacefully enjoying a cup of green tea on our back deck as we watched the squirrels moving about, hiding walnuts as they prepared for winter.

"Those squirrels are wise creatures. They plan without being in a hurry. They are not like some humans who wait till the last minute to make a plan and then find themselves acting out of panic," Julie observed.

I nodded my head in agreement as I slowly took another sip of refreshing tea.

Julie continued, "David, I have been thinking lately that we should be planning our funerals."

"Really?" I responded as a look of surprise crossed my face. "Sweetheart, I don't plan to leave this earth in the near future."

"David, that's just the point. We have time to plan our funerals now and to be as wise as the squirrels. Just think of the peace each of us will experience if we do it now, instead of having to do it under pressure later. This is the time to make plans and wise decisions, not when we are trying to handle our emotions at the time of the passing of one of us."

I sat back in my comfortable porch chair and pondered those words. Then I spoke, "Julie, that does make sense."

"David, we want our funerals to honor God for His great faithfulness to us."

"You're right. What a marvelous celebration we had on our 50th Wedding Anniversary. Our whole purpose was to give glory to God as well as to honor our many friends and family members who had impacted our lives for Him. What a glorious time we all had together. It was a superb celebration we will always remember!"

"Yes, and that happened because we planned it well ahead of time. Now we should do the same for our funerals."

"I agree. You know, Sweetheart, I not only married a beautiful lady but one who can truly think ten years ahead. That's one of the big reasons I married you."

Julie laughed, "Thank you for the compliment."

"Now tell me, Julie Leatherberry, what else have you been thinking regarding our funerals?"

"I'm glad you asked," she teased. "Well, we'll have to plan three funerals."

I looked puzzled, "And how can that be since there are only two of us?"

Julie grinned. "Well, we need to plan your funeral and my funeral, plus for a funeral if our Heavenly Father calls both of us home at the same time."

*Yes, sir,* I thought. *This wife of mine knows how to cover all the bases.*

I could not help but smile, "And I suppose you have already given some thought to what should be included in the funerals or funeral."

Julie chucked, "Actually, I have. How did you guess?"

"Easy, I know you after 57 years of marriage."

We both laughed.

"I've been waiting for the right time to speak to you about this. Watching the squirrels created the right opportunity to do so."

"So, Julie, what are some of your thoughts?"

Julie got up from the porch swing, walked toward me, bent down, and kissed my forehead.

"Sugar, are you trying to sweeten me up so I will accept your ideas?"

"Of course I am," she replied as she returned to the porch swing.

We both laughed again.

"Okay, tell me what you've been thinking."

"Well, you know how we love the song 'Find Us Faithful' sung by Steve Green. It has actually become one of our prayers."

Then Julie began to sing, "O may all who come behind us find us faithful. May the fire of our devotion light their way. May the footprints that we leave, lead them to believe, and the lives we live inspire them to obey. O may all who come behind us find us faithful."

I felt the Presence of our Lord as Julie sang those words.

"Yes, that is our prayer, and it must be sung at our funerals."

"And David, I know how much you love the great hymn, 'A Mighty Fortress is Our God' by Martin Luther. I think it also should be sung at your funeral or our combined funeral."

"Thank you, Sweetheart. This is a great start on planning our funerals."

I moved over to sit by Julie on the swing and took her hand. We bowed our heads and prayed, asking our Heavenly Father to carefully guide us in planning our funerals, for above all else we wanted Him glorified.

That night as I lay in bed by the side of my precious wife, who was already sleeping soundly, I whispered to God, *Heavenly Father, how marvelous it is that this jewel you have given me is so secure in you that she and I can joyfully plan our funerals. Thank you for the gift of Julie.*

I peacefully fell asleep as I whispered out loud, "Julie, my Love, I will love you forever."

*2018*

# MATURE MARRIAGE

One day after lunch in our home in Springfield, Julie and I got into a serious discussion that led to a big disagreement. Finally, Julie had had enough. She felt I was being stubborn in my refusal to accept her valid point of view.

In disgust she popped up out of her chair and began to march out of our kitchen. As she reached the doorway, she turned and emphatically announced, "It's a good thing we have a mature marriage!"

I shot back, "It sure is!" Then we both roared with laughter as I jumped up and dashed across the floor to give her a big hug. We had been married for more than fifty years. That was certainly plenty of time for our marriage to mature.

*    *    *

At another time Julie was doing the dishes and I sat nearby giving her moral support. As we talked, we soon got into a "vigorous" discussion.

Finally, Julie closed the debate by declaring, "David, you are welcome to your opinion, and I am welcome to mine, but I know which one is biblical!"

# KURDISTAN

The first week in December, 2019, I was pedaling on my stationary bike and reading *High Adventure in Tibet,* the life story of Victor Plymire. This passionate missionary walked across Tibet in the 1920s in the worst of conditions. As I read the last chapter, my heart was again set on fire for those who do not know the way to heaven.

"Oh, God," I cried out in deep anguish, "Please send Julie and me one more time to a people who have never heard the Good News. Of course I would like to go back to Afghanistan, the land of our calling, but for now, please send us to a place where the situation is more open and we would have more freedom to share the Good News. How can we stay in the States where the Gospel is easily available to anyone who wants to know the truth? Please don't let our ages, 77 and 78, stand in the way. You have given us good health. Please God, hear my cry!"

Soon it was Christmas Eve. Julie and I, along with her Aunt Lola and our friend Steve, attended a beautiful church service. When a young lady began to sing a Christmas song, it was as if someone turned on a video on a screen. For a minute or so I watched this vivid vision. Then, as suddenly as it had appeared, it finished. I was completely perplexed about the meaning.

The next morning, Christmas Day, I turned on my computer to check my email. There was a report from

Georg Taubmann, the International Director of Shelter Now International based in Germany. He wrote about the horrific suffering of Yazidi women at the hands of ISIS fighters. Now the vision I experienced the night before made sense. I knew Julie and I must go to offer healing and hope to the Yazidi refugees in Kurdistan in northern Iraq.

In December Julie had also read *High Adventure in Tibet*. She too had been deeply moved by the last chapter. God confirmed to Julie that it was His will that we reach out to the Yazidis. Together we prayed, believing He would make a way for us. He did. Our Assemblies of God World Missions Division agreed to loan us to Shelter Now International.

As always, Julie went into full-preparation mode. I marveled at her flexibility and joyful surrender to the Savior and His will. I thought about what I had often said, "If God wanted me to be a missionary, He had to give me Julie. Otherwise, I would still be in Ohio sitting under a big oak tree having dreams and visions but going nowhere, for Julie is the practical one who gets us there."

On March 9, 2020, we were packed and ready to fly to Erbil, Kurdistan, the next morning. Julie was excited. Early on the morning of March 9th she read in the Bible Psalm 37:34, *"Don't be impatient for the Lord to act! Travel steadily along his path...."* (NLT)*

*Wow!* Julie thought, *Tomorrow we travel! I can hardly wait.* Then we made a call to our future team members in Erbil, and everything suddenly changed. The coronavirus restrictions had begun closing down everything. It would be unwise for us to travel to Erbil.

*New Living Translation

Julie began weeping. Her heart was so set on being a blessing to the Yazidi girls. I telephoned her close friend Donna and asked her to please come to our place. She and her husband Steve immediately came. Julie was still crying when they arrived. Donna understood Julie's heart and embraced her.

Julie shared with Donna the verse she had read that morning. Donna accurately pointed out the words did not only mention travel, but the verse also said, *"Don't be impatient for the Lord to act!"* She encouraged Julie to be patient and to know that in time God would act. Then Donna prayed a Holy Spirit inspired prayer for Julie which gave my precious wife great comfort.

Donna's ministry to Julie touched my heart. I had seen Julie minister to many women, but it greatly blessed me to see someone like Donna minister to Julie. Sometimes others, myself included, think Julie is almost perfect. But she isn't. Like everyone else, at times, she needs to be ministered to.

One year later in 2021, the Lord opened the door, and we arrived in Erbil, Kurdistan, in northern Iraq. The day after we arrived was the official opening of the trauma center for Yazidi women sponsored by Shelter Now, although it had been unofficially open for several months. The center is located in Badraa, a small town.

At times tears slipped down our faces as we witnessed this inspiring event. The hall was filled with attractive smiling Yazidi young ladies. They were beautifully dressed for this special occasion. They were beginning to realize they are of great worth. One way or another all of them had been adversely

affected by the advance of ISIS. Some of them had
suffered unimaginable abuse by the ISIS men. After
the ceremony one young Yazidi woman wept on
Julie's shoulder. She had been horribly assaulted by
the fighters. Tears flowed because now she was in a
peaceful place and loved. Three weeks later Julie, with
other members of the staff, participated in a joyous
retreat for 25 of the Yazidi girls.

Later Julie assisted eight Yazidi women, most of
them husbandless, in a sewing course at the center.
Julie loved these ladies. One young widow had escaped
from ISIS with her three children. She had walked
five hours through a treacherous minefield carrying
her baby in her arms. She loved Julie. Her six-year-old
daughter adored Julie and always wanted to be with her.

For a period of time, Julie and I taught English
classes in Erbil three evenings a week. Our students
were educated Yazidis who did not live in the refugee
camps but had found places to live in Erbil. They were
mostly professional people who had lost everything
including their well-established houses in Syria.
They escaped with only their lives. They became our
dear friends who would invite us into their homes.
Often they asked vital questions about our Christian
faith. They had open hearts and open minds. They
appreciated the fact that the national Assembly of
God in Erbil, pastored by Ghassan Yalda, was glad to
provide rooms for the English classes.

After one year Julie and I felt we had fulfilled this
special assignment from our Heavenly Father, but it
was heart-wrenching to think of leaving. We would

especially miss Adeeb, the young man from Syria
who had wonderfully endeared himself to our hearts.
He had become our incredible personal assistant
and interpreter.

Near the end of our time in Kurdistan there was a
farewell for Julie at the Yazidi womens center. The women
she had helped teach came to the center, especially to say
goodbye. One of the things Julie mentioned to them was
that although God had not given her biological daughters,
she had spiritual daughters in different countries. Julie
named the countries.

There was a quiet pause. Then one of the women
spoke words that sunk deep into Julie's heart, always to be
remembered. She said, "We will be your Iraqi daughters."

*Springfield, Missouri 2022*

# SPIRITUAL SONS AND DAUGHTERS

Julie and I strolled hand in hand in the magnificent
botanical garden enjoying the beautiful flowers. As we
walked around the small lake we stopped and perched
ourselves on a wooden bench. The ducks swam up as if
they knew us. After a few minutes of quietness, I said
to Julie, "I'm happy for our missionary friends who are
now grandparents. It's wonderful to see how they rejoice
over their children and grandchildren."

Julie responded, "Yes, that's great. It's humorous
how they are always ready to show us their pictures."

We both chuckled.

Delightfully Julie said, "David, God in His wisdom chose not to give us biological children, but He also chose in His wisdom to give us spiritual children. You know, David, that's biblical. The Apostle Paul called Timothy and Titus his sons. The Apostle Peter called Mark his son."

I reflected on Julie's words. The Lord knew I never wanted to replace the biological fathers of my spiritual sons. In fact, I had often prayed with them for their fathers. The Lord also knew I carefully checked my own heart to make sure I was not responding to them out of a need to have sons. Many years ago Julie had confirmed to me that my motives were right in having spiritual sons as well as spiritual daughters. She knew how to read my heart and would be honest with me. At times she saved me from making mistakes and corrected me when I needed it. That enabled me to trust her judgment when she affirmed and confirmed me.

"Julie," I said, "I've always marveled how you knew how to relate to our spiritual sons. You brought a dimension into their lives that was not possible for me to do."

"Well, David, that is also true of you regarding our spiritual daughters."

I sat back on the bench and took a deep breath as I pondered Julie's words. Yes, Julie and I are extremely blessed to have such children. It has been an incredible joy to encourage and facilitate them. I thought about the African proverb, *The man I woke up passed me on the way*. We feel that way about our spiritual children.

*Springfield, Missouri 2022*

# GRATEFUL

It was our 58th wedding anniversary. Julie was 79 and I had turned 80. To celebrate we went to a quaint country restaurant. We had reserved a room just for us that was beautifully decorated with antiques and pictures from the 1950s. This brought back nostalgic memories of the days of our childhood and teenage years. It was a quiet place. The staff treated us with great respect. The candlelight danced as it reflected off the wall. Most of all, I delighted in seeing the light's reflection in Julie's beautiful brown eyes, the eyes I loved to look into from the day I fell in love with this radiant, godly girl.

We took our time as we enjoyed the exquisite food. I told Julie all the many reasons I loved her. In 58 years, I never once doubted that I had married the right girl. She felt the same way about me. We often say our marriage was made in heaven, and that it is the little heaven to go to the big heaven in. It was exciting to know our beautiful relationship would last forever in heaven. We realized that death would someday come to each of us, but we would be separated for only a little while.

Julie, with her winsome smile that was enhanced by small emerging wrinkles, began telling me why she loved me. I reached across the table and held her hand as tears of gratitude slowly slipped down my cheeks. I had learned more about the love of Christ from Julie than anyone else. She completely loved me, knowing me better than anyone else. She knew my faults and weaknesses, and yet she still loved me.

Later that night we knelt and prayed together by our bed as we did 58 years ago on our wedding night when we committed our marriage to the Lord Jesus Christ. Our hearts overflowed with gratitude as we thanked Christ, the center of our marriage, for His unwavering faithfulness to us. I especially thanked Him for Julie, who will always be *Julie, my love.*

# OTHER BOOKS BY
# DAVID LEATHERBERRY

*Afghanistan, My Tears*

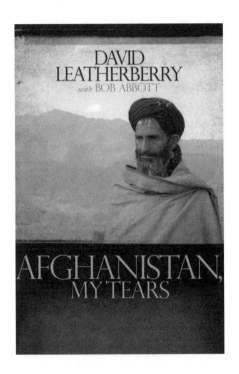

A compelling story of one couple's deep love for the people of Afghanistan. Though danger and chaos were their constant companions, neither could keep this couple from answering God's summons to give their lives in service to the Afghans.

*Abdul & Mr. Friday*

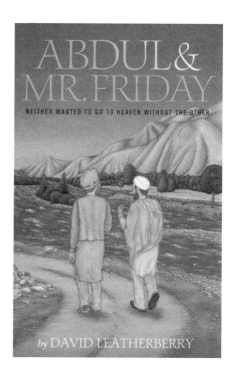

This book is an account based on a true story about a devout Muslim and a dedicated Christian. Each was willing to die for the other, yet neither could be moved from his faith. These were two men from two different worlds whose bond of friendship could not be broken. Neither wanted to go to heaven without the other.

*Strength from Inspiring Stories*

These nineteen short stories are intriguing and insightful. The diversity of the narratives is inviting to all ages from childhood to elderly veterans. At times you will find tears in the stories from which hope arises.

# HOW TO ORDER

These books as well as *Julie, My Love* are available at $10 each including shipping & handling.

Please make checks and money orders payable to:

Enhearten Books
3938 W. Madison Place
Springfield, MO 65802

The books can be purchased as e-books on Amazon.

If you would like to correspond with the author, please use this email address: enheartenbooks@gmail.com

David would be delighted to hear from you.